Mastering the Power of

P

Aldus Persuasion 2.0

Roger C. Parker

Dow Jones-Irwin
Homewood, Illinois 60430

© RICHARD D. IRWIN, INC., 1990

Dow Jones-Irwin is a trademark of Dow Jones & Company, Inc.

Sponsoring editor: Susan Glinert Stevens, Ph.D.
Project editor: Karen Nelson
Production manager: Diane Palmer
Cover design: Image House
Printer: R. R. Donnelley & Sons Company

Library of Congress Cataloging-in-Publication Data

Parker, Roger C.
    Mastering the power of Aldus Persuasion 2.0 / Roger C. Parker.
        p.   cm.
    Includes bibliographical references (p.
    Includes index.
    ISBN 1–55623–243–8
    1. Aldus Persuasion (Computer program) 2. Business
    presentations—Graphic methods—Data processing. I. Title.
HF5718.22P37   1990
808.5′1′02855369—dc20   90–3323
                                           CIP

Printed in the United States of America

1 2 3 4 5 6 7 8 9 0 DO 7 6 5 4 3 2 1 0

The author extends special thanks to Stephen Hale and the staff at DesignAd, a desktop publishing design firm located in Marina del Rey, California.

Mastering the Power of Aldus Persuasion is dedicated to everyone who initially feared facing their first audience—and later found out that it was one of the most exciting and pleasurable experiences they ever had.

Contents

Introduction   1

Chapter One:
Overview   9

Chapter Two:
Planning your presentation strategy   31

Chapter Three:
Formatting your presentation   75

Chapter Four:
Adding, editing and formatting text   123

Chapter Five:
Using charts, graphs and tables to
bring numbers to life   191

Chapter Six:
Creating persuasive drawings   227

Chapter Seven:
Advanced techniques   275

Chapter Eight:
Reorganizing and reformatting
your presentations   295

Chapter Nine:
Preparing speaker's notes and
audience handouts   307

Chapter Ten:
Output considerations   323

Chapter Eleven:
Presentation tips   369

Bibliography   387

Index   391

Introduction

The purpose of this book is to describe a simple, stress-free, six step procedure for creating effective presentations. Regardless of how much, or how little, computer experience you may have had, Aldus Persuasion can help you prepare effective good-looking slides, overheads, flip-charts and on-screen presentations which will help you inform, motivate and persuade others.

Aldus Persuasion is a very flexible, highly personal software program.

You can use Aldus Persuasion at whatever level you find most comfortable. You can get started very quickly, producing your first presentation within hours of Persuasion's arrival in your office. Although it's easy to get started, Persuasion, however, offers tremendous flexibility. Aldus Persuasion can grow with you. As your presentation needs become more and more sophisticated, you can begin to use more and more of Persuasion's capabilities. You will probably never outgrow the power built into Aldus Persuasion.

When its capacities are used to their fullest extent, Persuasion can create slides and overheads which can "knock the socks off" of even the most jaded audience.

Steps to success

There are six basic steps involved in creating a successful presentation with Aldus Persuasion. This book has been organized around those steps. They are:

1. Choose the right media
2. Organize and edit your ideas
3. Format your slides and overheads
4. Add emphasis to words
5. Enhance your ideas with visuals
6. Prepare notes and handouts

After you've developed your presentation on the basis of the six steps outlined above, all that remains is to rehearse your presentation and check-out last-minute details—like making sure that back-up projector bulbs are going to be available. Needless to say, the more advance preparation you do, the smoother your presentation will proceed.

Chapter One consists of an overview of Persuasion's capabilities and an introduction to some of the terms and concepts used throughout the book. We pay special attention to features which have been added in Persuasion 2.0, and versions that follow. These greatly enhance Persuasion's capabilities.

In the chapters that follow, we carefully consider each of the six steps.

Step One: Choose the right media

In Chapter Two, we start by taking a brief look at the various presentation media available. Aldus Persuasion is equally at home producing 35mm slides, black and white or color overhead transparencies, flip-charts or computer-based on-screen presentations. Each option offers important advantages which Persuasion can help you take full advantage of. Each media also has disadvantages which you should be aware of before you move forward.

Step Two: Organize and edit your ideas

Aldus Persuasion offers you a new way of preparing a presentation. Instead of viewing your presentation as a "speech," Persuasion allows you to view your presentation as a developing partnership between outline, notes, audience handouts and slides or overheads.

Persuasion's Outline view lets you work the way you want to work. Persuasion accommodates you, whether you prefer working in a methodical, step-by-step manner or whether you like to enthusiastically brainstorm new ideas and organize them later. Aldus Persuasion is based on its outline capabilities. Persuasion's powerful Outline view makes it easy for you to quickly get started, yet never have to discard or re-do work. Ideas entered into a Persuasion outline automatically appear in slides and overheads, without re-typing. Later, as you edit the text on individual slides, your outline will be automatically updated.

Step Three: Format your slides and overheads

In Chapter Three, we begin to design your presentation. We look at how Persuasion's combination of AutoTemplates and Slide masters permits you to create high-impact slides and overheads which are consistent enough to provide slide-to-slide consistency—creating a family resemblance between each slide or overhead—yet flexible enough to accommodate the different demands of different slide and overhead content.

Persuasion's Slide masters make it easy to add text and graphic elements which will automatically appear on each slide. These Slide masters also allow you to pre-format the subtlest text and graphic details. This frees you from starting from scratch, re-choosing text attributes or chart types each time you use them.

Step Four: Add emphasis to words

In Chapter Four, we take a closer look at ways to format text. We'll see how Persuasion's Slide masters allow you to determine in advance how words entered in the Outline view will look on a finished slide or overhead. We'll show how to create Slide master placeholders which will allow you to precisely position and format all aspects of Slide titles and supporting copy.

Step Five: Enhance your ideas with visuals

Chapters Five and Six are devoted to visuals. In Chapter Five, we'll look at how to use Persuasion's powerful built-in charting and graphing tools. Persuasion makes it easy to translate numbers into impressive charts and graphs. These numbers can be typed into Persuasion's Data sheet, or you can import data from existing spreadsheets. We'll see how easy it is to pre-format charts and graphs, which will save you hours of work.

In Chapter Six, we take a closer look at Persuasion's drawing tools and some of the techniques which can be used to enhance previously-created drawings—including clip art.

Step Six: Prepare notes and handouts

There's more to producing a presentation than creating good-looking slides and overheads. As a presenter, you need notes to help you both rehearse and deliver your presentation. Your audience also has needs which extend beyond the presentation. Persuasion makes it easy to prepare attractive, readable hand-out materials which will remind your audience how good your presentation was. These handouts add tangibility to your presentation, making it easy for your audience to review important points covered during the presentation.

Rehearsals

Rehearsals are the final step in presentation production. Before you stand up in front of a group, you should be thoroughly comfortable with the material you're going to present. The goal is not to become an "actor reading a script," but to develop sufficient familiarity with the material so you'll know how to pace your presentation.

Together, these steps create an organized sequence of events which can take a lot of the stress out of sharing your knowledge and enthusiasm with others. These steps make it easy to build upon your audience's pre-disposition to see you succeed (described in Chapter Ten).

At every step in the process, we have included numerous checklists and worksheets which will help you relate Persuasion's capabilities to your unique presentation needs.

Requirements

Because Aldus Persuasion is designed for use on Apple Macintosh computers, you already have a head-start on learning the program. Persuasion uses many of the commands common to many Apple Macintosh software programs. Thus, you probably already know how to open and save files, etc. (If you just purchased a Macintosh, you might want to spend a few days getting familiar with it before moving on.)

Before beginning work with Persuasion, you should also be comfortable with Macintosh features like the Clipboard and Scrapbook as well as the all-important differences between "Cut" and "Clear." ("Cut" places text and graphics into memory, so you can "Paste" them into a different location. "Clear" eliminates highlighted text and graphics from the computer's memory.) You should be comfortable with the idea of selecting a graphic by clicking on it or dragging the cursor through a text block to highlight it.

Although Aldus Persuasion can be used with Macintosh Plus and Macintosh SE, it really comes into its own on a Macintosh II series computer equipped with a color monitor. (In Chapter Three, we'll show you how you can create color slides using black and white monitors.)

Like all software programs, Aldus Persuasion benefits from added memory and hard disk storage capacity. Extra memory allows faster operation and faster manipulation and movement of larger graphic images.

Access to clip-art and additional typefaces will allow you extra flexibility. It's important that you choose the typefaces most suitable for your printers.

Output devices

Aldus Persuasion can work with a variety of output devices, including black and white laser printers, high-resolution typesetters, color ink-jet or thermal printers as well as film recorders. Equally important, Persuasion's slide files can be sent to service bureaus like Autographics, Genigraphics or Crossfield-Dicomed for completion. These options are described in Chapter Ten, "Output Alternatives."

Desktop publishing versus desktop presentations

On the surface, Aldus Persuasion may appear to be simply an extension of the basic concepts involved in the "desktop publishing revolution." Aldus Persuasion and desktop publishing programs like Aldus PageMaker are similar in that they both give individuals with ideas the power they need to share those ideas with others.

Although many use desktop publishing programs to create slide and overhead presentations, desktop publishing programs reveal significant compromises when compared to Aldus Persuasion which was designed from the beginning to enhance the presentation process.

Here are some of the significant differences between desktop publishing and desktop presentation programs:

- Desktop publishing programs do not integrate the process of developing ideas with the process of formatting the appearance of a presentation.
- Desktop publishing programs do not integrate the production of notes and audience handouts with the presentation planning process.
- Desktop publishing programs do not allow the use of multiple template masters within a project.
- Desktop publishing programs do not make it easy to reorganize the sequence of slides nor do they allow you to share slides and overheads between different projects.
- Desktop publishing programs do not allow computer-based, on-screen presentations.

With the introduction of Version 2.0, Aldus Persuasion has moved even farther towards becoming your ideal presentation partner. Persuasion Version 2.0 offers more advanced video effects as well as integrates the preparation of notes with the outlining process.

At one time or another, nearly everyone has to speak in front of a group. Regardless whether you work for yourself, a small company, or a Fortune 500 firm, your career success is often based on your ability to inform and motivate others.

In the pages that follow, you'll learn how Aldus Persuasion can help you translate your ideas into presentations that your audience will enjoy—instead of tolerate.

Roger C. Parker

Dover, New Hampshire

Chapter One: Overview

Aldus Persuasion makes it easy to look your best in front of an audience. Aldus Persuasion helps you prepare good-looking slides and overheads that will simultaneously impress your audience and boost your confidence. Persuasion's power comes from its ability to guide you through the entire process of planning, creating and presenting your ideas to others. Here is a brief overview of those Persuasion features which make it easy to look your best in front of an audience.

"Does the thought of standing up in front of a group and talking scare you?"

If so, you're not alone. Research indicates that fear of public speaking is one of the most widespread anxieties people share. Yet, regardless of whether you work for yourself, a large corporation, a government agency or a non-profit agency or association, your business and professional success is often directly related to your ability to stand up in front of a group and inform, motivate or persuade others.

That's where Aldus Persuasion comes in. Aldus Persuasion makes it easy to look your best in front of an audience. Aldus Persuasion is an integrated software program which makes it easy to organize your ideas and present them to others as high-impact slides and overheads. These attractive visuals play an important role in boosting your self confidence.

You'll find that your worries about the effectiveness of your presentation will recede to the extent that you know that you're armed with good-looking slides and overheads which will support your ideas.

Here is a brief overview of some of the more important Persuasion tools which will help you translate your ideas and knowledge into good-looking slides and overheads

Built-in outlining

One of the ironies of the personal computing revolution is the way that often the latest high-tech tools are used to implement the basic tools and techniques of effective communication. And one of the most effective tools is the importance of preparing strong outlines. Outlines make it easy to brainstorm—to quickly get ideas out of your brain and onto paper, where they can be massaged and re-organized until they say exactly what you want to say in as few words as possible.

Persuasion makes it easy to plan your presentation by making it easy to outline your ideas and re-organize your slides and overheads. Working with Persuasion's Outline view, you can easily present even the most complicated presentations as a series of slide titles with multiple levels of subheads.

Creating an outline is as easy as typing. You use the Tab and Delete keys to change the levels of indented, subordinate information.

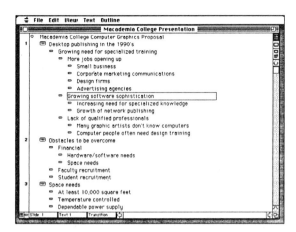

Persuasion's Outline view. Note that "Growing software sophistication" has been selected in its original position.

You can easily insert new ideas at any point or re-organize the sequence of your slides or overheads. You can move words or phrases from one level to another or move them from one slide to another.

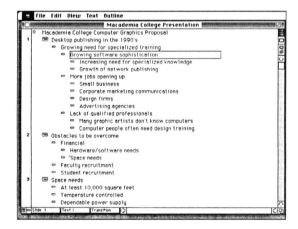

Repositioned "Growing software sophistication" in its new location.

When you move a phrase, all the subordinate levels associated with it automatically follow.

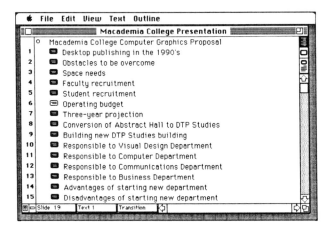

Collapsed outlines show just slide titles.

Persuasion permits you to easily collapse your outline so you can get an overall picture of your presentation by viewing just the slide titles, then expand your outline to view the details.

Persuasion now allows you to select more than one section of an outline and move them to new locations. You can easily create a new slide, for example, based on ideas which were originally located in four, or more, other slides.

Subtitles can also be added to outlines. These subtitles will automatically be placed in their proper location on slides and overheads which contain a subtitle placeholder on the Slide master.

AutoTemplates

While you are working in the Outline view, organizing and reorganizing words, Persuasion is working in the background, automatically formatting your presentation. Once you have established a format for your presentation, Persuasion will automatically format your words and visuals—freeing you to concentrate on content. Persuasion will automatically be formatting the appearance of your slides and overheads by choosing appropriate background colors, borders, and accents—like shadows—needed to add impact to your presentation.

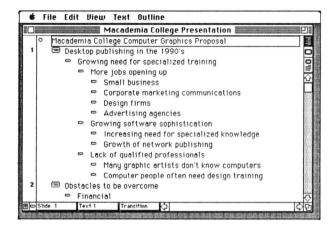

While you are adding, removing or reorganizing text in Outline view...

For example, while you are concentrating on choosing the right words for each slide or overhead, Persuasion will be automatically choosing: typeface, type size, type style, indents, alignment—flush-left, flush-right, centered or justified—color and graphic enhancements (like bullets, check-marks or asterisks) for each level of detail you're including in your slides.

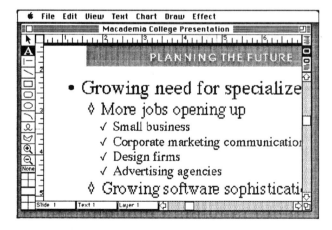

...Persuasion is formatting your ideas in the background, as this Slide view shows.

Persuasion's AutoTemplates not only make it easy to format your presentation, they also make it easy to maintain slide-to-slide and overhead-to-overhead consistency. Added to Version 2.0 is the ability to apply different AutoTemplates to existing presentations.

Multiple Slide masters

Often, your presentation will contain a mixture of slide types. Persuasion makes it easy for you to assign multiple Slide masters to your presentation.

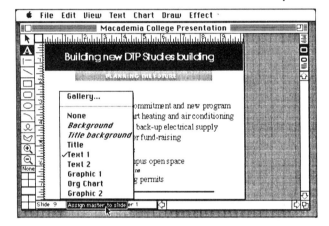

Screen shot illustrating bottom-up menu listing Slide masters

You can easily assign a different Slide master for each type of slide (or overhead) likely to be included in your presentation.

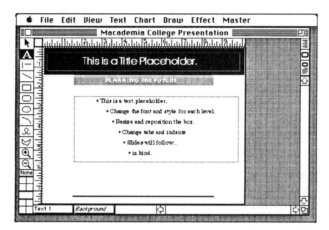

Slide master with text placeholders

One Slide master for slides which are primarily text-oriented.

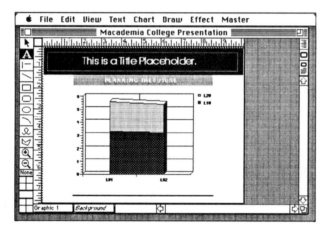

Slide master for area chart placeholder

Another Slide master might be be based around a previously-formatted type of chart or graph.

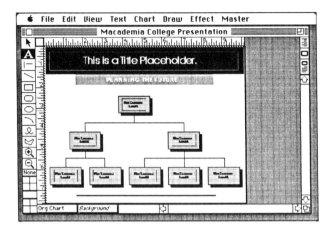

Screen shot of organization chart

Still another format might be based on a previously-formatted organization chart.

The ability to create multiple Slide masters, each with fully formatted borders, background colors and text is not only a great time-saver, but ensures consistency throughout your presentation. Slide masters may be added or changed at any time, further speeding your work.

In addition to allowing you to create multiple Slide masters for each presentation, Persuasion 2.0, (and following), makes it easy for you to share slide masters between presentations. Slide masters for individual types of slides from a "New Business" presentation, for example, can be easily used as the basis for individual slides in a "Year End Projections" presentation.

Built-in charting and graphing

Persuasion's built-in charting and graphing capabilities make it easy to translate numbers into charts and graphs. A variety of chart and graph types are built in. These include not only bar, pie and line charts, but also high-low and scatter charts.

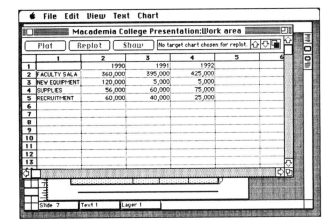

Use Persuasion's Data sheet to enter information for charts, graphs and tables.

Persuasion includes a Data sheet matrix for you to directly enter the data you want to display. Simply enter the information you want to display in the appropriate rows and columns, and Persuasion will do the rest! Or, you can directly import data from spreadsheets previously created with other spreadsheet programs, like Microsoft Excel.

Because Persuasion allows you to import data from previously-created spreadsheets, you don't have to re-enter data. This saves time and increases accuracy.

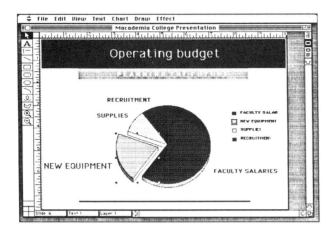

You can easily enhance charts and graphs by separately formatting individual segments or textblocks.

Once created, you can selectively enhance, or reformat, all, or part, of the text included in a chart or graph. You can also overlay charts and graphs.

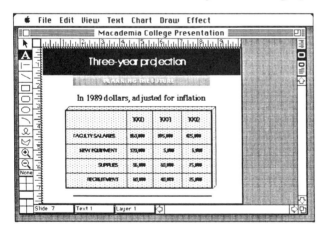

Persuasion creates tables which make it easy to display and compare complicated information.

You can also present information in table form. In addition to speed, Persuasion allows you to separately format X and Y axis information, highlight individual columns or rows—as well as sequentially introduce them.

Builds

One of Persuasion's most powerful features is its ability to allow you to work in layers. Each Slide master can include multiple layers, permitting you to assemble builds. Builds permit the *progressive display* of information.

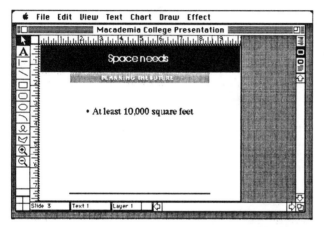

Persuasion's builds permit you to introduce information one step...

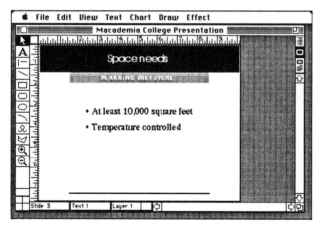

...at a time.

Instead of distracting your audience by showing a full list, you can reveal each item as you discuss it.

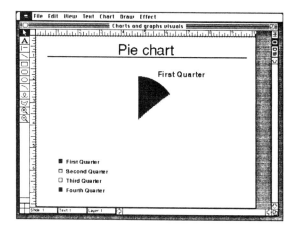

Charts, too, can be introduced one segment...

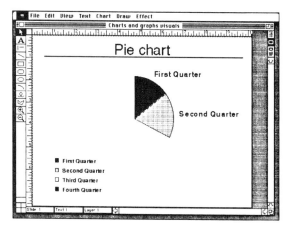

...at a time.

Likewise, instead of showing a completed pie chart, you can show each segment of the chart as you introduce it. Again, this feature permits you to focus your audience's attention on the content of your presentation, as you introduce each new point.

Tables, too, can be built on a row-by-row or column-by-column basis.

Transitions

One of Persuasion Version 2.0's most powerful new features is the way it allows you to control the way the slides replace each other during on-screen electronic presentations using Persuasion's Slide show feature. Instead of abruptly switching from slide to slide, (like a slide projector does), Persuasion allows dramatic segues between slides similar to professional video animations or high-quality television productions.

Among the transition effects Persuasion 2.0, (and following), offers are:

- **Wipes.** This is where new slides appear to push the previous slide off the screen from top (or bottom), from left (or right), or appear from the center of the screen.

- **Blinds.** Horizontal or vertical "blinds" in existing slides open to reveal the next slide.

- **Glitters.** The new slide is revealed by a multitude of small squares which cascade across the screen from top to bottom or diagonally from top left to bottom right.

- **Dissolves.** Numerous small squares throughout the entire screen open to reveal the next slide.

Persuasion's new transition effects can be applied either between individual slides or between layers of individual slides revealed one at a time. Indeed, Persuasion 2.0, (and following), allows you to apply one transition type between slides and use a different type of transition between layers—or builds—of individual slides.

Drawing tools

Aldus Persuasion includes numerous drawing tools. You can enhance your presentation with a variety of rules, boxes as well as create illustrations from scratch. Persuasion's drawing tools equal those of dedicated drawing programs.

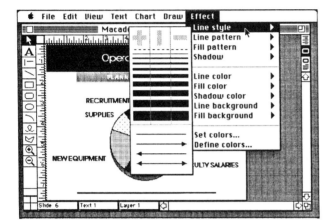

You can choose different line thicknesses for horizontal and vertical lines.

You can create lines of different lengths and add end-caps at either, or both ends. These can be used to create call-out's—brief phrases which draw attention to important points.

You can also import and enhance clip-art or graphic files previously prepared with programs like Aldus FreeHand or Adobe Illustrator 88. This has many implications, especially in teaching applications.

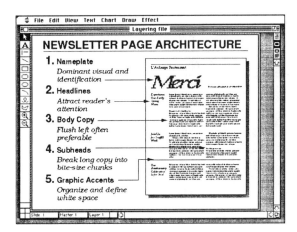

You can include PageMaker pages saved as EPS files on overhead transparencies created with Persuasion.

For example, if you are teaching graphic design, you can import a previously-prepared PageMaker page and draw attention to important aspects of it with arrows and call-outs.

In addition, Persuasion 2.0, (and following), incorporates a more powerful polygon drawing tool. This allows you to draw multi-sided objects and easily modify them after they have been created. Persuasion will even help you create a complex multi-sided object by automatically joining the starting and ending points of your drawing with far more accuracy than you could probably do yourself. Simply triple-click at any point and Persuasion will do the rest.

Grouping and ungrouping

Another Persuasion feature you're likely to appreciate is the ability to group and ungroup graphic images. You can use this feature to selectively emphasize portions of a drawing, a chart or a graph.

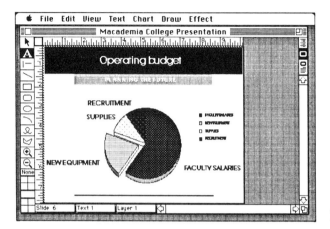

By ungrouping a chart, you can selectively enhance any portion of it.

For example, after creating a pie chart, you can select the most important segment—or one segment at a time—for extra emphasis by pulling it away from the rest of the chart.

Grouping permits you to accurately resize and reposition several graphic elements at once or lock call-out's to imported graphics.

Reorganizing your presentation

Persuasion's Slide show and Slide sorter features make it easy to change the order of your presentation.

The Slide show feature permits you to preview your presentation from the audience's perspective. After you have created your presentation, you can watch the slides or overheads automatically appear on the screen of your computer in correct order. This makes it easy to check that slides and overheads follow each other in a logical progression.

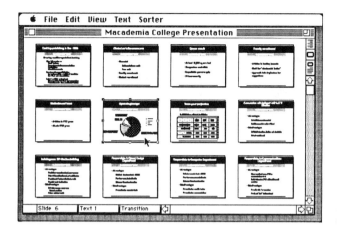

Note the original location of the pie chart in Persuasion's Slide sorter view.

Persuasion's Slide sorter view permits you to change the order of your slides and overheads. Depending on the size of your monitor, you can view all, or most, of the slides you have prepared at reduced size. Working in this view, you simply "grab" a slide and move it to a new location.

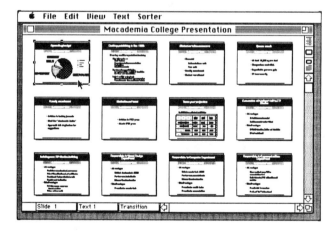

The pie chart is now the first slide.

As you reorganize slide sequence in the Slide sorter view, Persuasion automatically updates and renumbers your outline, notes and handouts. Slide sorter views can be actual size, or reduced to 66, 33 or 20 percent. Larger sizes show more detail, smaller sizes include more slides.

Color capabilities

Persuasion is equally at home working in color or black and white. Indeed, because Persuasion allows you to choose colors based on their name, you can actually create color presentations using a Macintosh SE or Macintosh II with a black and white monitor.

Of course, if you have a Macintosh II with a color monitor, you have even more options. You can mix your own custom colors, carefully controlling not only color balance but also the color brightness and saturation.

Color overheads can be easily produced in your office using color ink-jet printers like the Hewlett-Packard PaintJet or color thermal printers like those made by Tektronix or QMS. Color slides can be produced with film recorders like the Montage FR-1.

Or, you can send your files to service bureaus like AutoGraphix, Genigraphics or Crossfield-Dicomed for overnight or forty-eight hour slide production. If you have a modem connected to your computer, you can send your files over the telephone lines. Or, you can send floppy diskettes containing files of your presentation.

Presentation aids

Persuasion also helps you deliver your presentation. In addition to helping you create effective, good-looking slides and overheads, Persuasion makes it easy to prepare speaker's notes as well as audience handouts. Speaker's notes contain a reduced-size reproduction of a slide plus the points you want to emphasize during your presentation. Handouts contain reduced-size reproductions of 1, 2, 3, 4 or

6 slides. Notes and handouts can be numbered, dated, and personalized with the presenter's or audience's name and date of presentation.

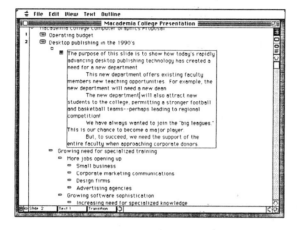

Persuasion 2.0 permits you to create speaker's notes while preparing your outline.

One of the most exciting additions to Version 2.0, (and following), is the ability to prepare speaker's notes while outlining your presentation. Persuasion offers you a direct link between your outline and the speaker's notes pages. This means you can write notes to yourself, (or another presenter), reminding yourself, (or the presenter) of points to emphasize *while the ideas are fresh,* while developing your outline.

In addition, Persuasion allows you to automatically format your outlines for maximum visual impact. Each level of your outline can be formatted in a different typeface, type size and/or type style. This permits you to use your outlines as additional handouts which will reinforce the impact of your presentation after it has been completed.

Persuasion text-handling tools include a built-in spell-checker which will help you avoid embarrassing errors. Also included is a powerful search and replace capability which can save you hours of work, should the name of the product you're preparing a presentation describing be changed at the last minute!

Convenience features

Persuasion 2.0's convenience features include a vastly-expanded repertoire of keyboard shortcuts. These make it easier to edit and format text and—in Slide show mode—to advance layer by layer or slide by slide through your presentation. You can also pause, go backwards or go directly to any desired slide. You can also add an on-screen cursor to your presentation, blank the screen, or allow the screen to darken while you stop to discuss a particular point or answer a question from the audience.

Zooming in and out

Another feature added to Persuasion 2.0, (and following), includes the ability to view your slides and overheads at various degrees of magnification.

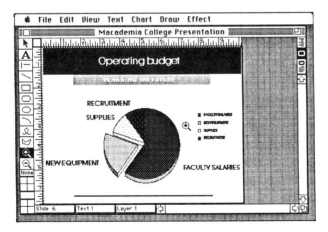

You can view the complete slide...

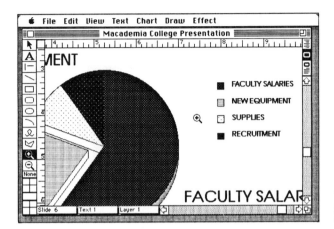

...or view just a portion of it at greatly increased size.

The new Zoom feature allows you to focus your attention on a greatly magnified section of an individual slide, or slowly back off to full "fit in screen" size. This makes it easy to work with exacting detail on small details and then back off to observe how those changes relate to the entire slide.

You can toggle between increasing or decreasing image size by holding down the Shift key while clicking on your slide or overhead using the Zoom up or Zoom down tools. Note that the position of the tool remains in the same slide location as you change image size.

Review and looking forward...

The above are just a few of the features which make Persuasion such an easy-to-use, but powerful tool. Additional Persuasion features will be introduced at appropriate points.

In the chapters which follow, we'll see how these tools can be put to work creating a variety of slides and overheads. We'll start by analyzing the dynamics of presentation planning and then look at how Persuasion's AutoTemplates and Slide master features make it easy to format your presentation.

Chapter Two:
Planning your presentation strategy

Choosing an appropriate presentation strategy is based on the interplay of message, audience and environment. Choosing the proper presentation media involves planning. You should be aware of the advantages and disadvantages of the various presentation media available. After choosing the appropriate media, you should begin planning the sequential introduction of information. Persuasion's built-in outlining capability helps you focus your efforts and organize your ideas, making it easy to translate your communication goals into good-looking, logically-presented slides and overheads.

There are two steps involved in planning your presentation strategy. The first step involves choosing the proper presentation media. Aldus Persuasion is equally at home preparing 35mm slides, overhead transparencies, flip-charts or computer-based on-screen presentations.

Next, you should organize your ideas. Chances are, you may be a bit overwhelmed by the great amount of information you'd like to share with others. Not to worry! Persuasion's Outline view helps you edit and organize your ideas. Best of all, by organizing your presentation in Persuasion's Outline view, you won't have to re-enter the text when you create your actual slides and overheads.

Step One: Choosing your presentation media

The first step in creating a powerful presentation is to determine the proper presentation media. The proper media is determined by several factors, including:

- Available time and budget resources
- Audience size
- Desired audience involvement
- Length of presentation
- Room lighting
- Convenience

35mm slides

Time and budget resources will likely play a major role in determining the format of your presentation. When time and budget permits, 35mm slides are the best choice. Color slides permit dramatic presentations. Your words and numbers can dramatically appear in color against a dark background. Crisp, color-saturated charts and drawings can be included. In addition, 35mm slides permit you to enhance your presentation by utilizing advanced techniques like builds—where your ideas progressively build upon each other.

The relatively recent introduction of affordable slide production services also makes slides an excellent choice. As described in Chapter Nine, "Output Alternatives," you can send Persuasion files to a slide production service for overnight—or near-overnight—conversion into 35mm slides. Your files can be physically mailed or sent by courier to the slide production facility, or you can use a modem to instantaneously transmit your files to the production facility.

Costs will be far less than what the same slides would have previously cost if the slides were created from scratch.

If you have a film recorder, you can easily produce your own 35mm slides. A film recorder is basically a combination of a computer screen plus a 35mm camera. Film recorders connect directly to your computer. Film recorders give you complete control over your production, although you still have to develop the slides and put them in slide mounts. Because of their low unit cost, film recorders offer the least-expensive way to prepare slides—although a lot of volume is needed to justify the initial investment required.

The primary disadvantage of slides is that they require a darkened room. As room lighting levels increase, the effectiveness of slides tends to decrease.

Convenience and security are additional factors to consider. If your presentation involves travel, your presentation can easily fit in a Kodak Carousel slide tray. These are small and light enough to easily be hand-carried on airplanes. An added virtue of the Carousel format is that it is virtually impossible to get your slides out of order. If you drop the Carousel, the slides won't fall out.

There are several disadvantages related to fact that 35mm slides work best in darkened rooms.

- Presentations based on 35mm slides must be short, as your audience is unlikely to want to sit in the dark all day.
- Darkened rooms make it difficult for your audience to take notes.
- Darkened rooms inhibit speaker/audience interaction. It's difficult to gauge audience reaction or acknowledge audience comments and questions.
- Slide presentations are relatively inflexible. You

cannot easily add or eliminate slides during your presentation, based on timing and audience response.

Overhead transparencies

Overheads overcome the problems associated with the need for darkened rooms. Overheads can be quickly and economically produced. Overheads can be prepared just moments before a presentation is scheduled to begin, facilitating last-minute changes.

Overheads offer a lot of flexibility. You can easily insert or remove selected overheads during your presentation, based on how time is running as well as audience reactions. You might even prepare extra overheads which will only be used if the audience asks a relevant question.

Blank overheads can be written on with colored markers during your presentation.

Overheads work effectively under a wide range of lighting conditions. This avoids the "prisoner" complex an audience can get while trapped in a darkened room for too long. Overheads can be used under normal room lighting, so they can be used for day-long presentations, although legibility and color saturation improves as light levels are decreased. Try to avoid lighting which falls directly on the screen.

HELPFUL HINT

You can enhance the appearance of overheads by slightly reducing lighting levels at just the front of a room, leaving normal room illumination in the remainder of the room. This improves reproduction quality and makes it easy to maintain eye contact with your audience.

Overheads can be either black and white or color.

- Black and white overheads can be printed on a laser printer, or you can use an office copier to make overheads from original artwork prepared with a laser or ink-jet printer.

- A new generation of relatively low-cost color printers are now available. These include the Hewlett-Packard PaintJet and faster PaintJet XC as well as thermal color printers from firms like QMS and Tektronix.

Overheads lack some of the drama and flexibility of 35mm slides. For example, you can't easily include builds without "overhead flopping." Another disadvantage of overheads is that it is relatively easy for them to get out of order. If you drop the folder containing your overheads on the way into the conference room, you might have to reorganize your presentation just moments before you give it!

Computer-based presentations

If you have access to a computer, your presentation can be delivered right off the screen. If your audience consists of four to six key people, a large screen monitor might be sufficient.

Many seminar facilities and teaching facilities have video projectors with large screens which can be viewed by larger audiences. In some installations, multiple monitors are used. One computer at the front of the room could drive numerous monitors placed strategically throughout the room. People in the back row could see your presentation as well as people in the front of the room.

Computer-based presentations offer the advantage of advanced video techniques. For example, Version 2.0 of Persuasion offers a variety of transition effects, including dissolves and wipes. When used in conjunction with builds, you can create a very animated presentation. Remote controls often allow you to walk around the room while controlling your presentation.

The only disadvantage of on-screen presentations is that the attention of your audience is likely to be focused more on the monitors than on you.

A relatively new development involves the video projector pads. These are placed on top of an overhead projector, in place of transparencies. The advantage of projector pads is that they concentrate the audience's attention at the front of the room. They are relatively small and lightweight.

The disadvantages of projector pads involve logistics, cost, performance and reliability. First, projector pads require that a computer be present. This means you have to make sure that a computer—and a backup—are going to be available for your presentation. Sometimes, the performance of these units isn't up to the level of conventional transparencies. The images are often not as brilliant as overheads. Occasionally, there is shadowing— where faint outlines of previous slides appear on the screen.

Perhaps reliability is the biggest disadvantage of on-screen units. They are easily damaged by dropping, which means you might want to make sure a back-up unit is available if you're taking yours with you on an airplane—or across town. Because of heat build-up, most projector pads include a fan. You may find the fan's noise and wind currents distracting and the noise may be picked-up by a microphone.

A final disadvantage is the fact that most are presently limited to black and white.

HELPFUL HINT

It is impossible to overestimate the importance of back-up's. Never allow a hardware malfunction to destroy your presentation before it begins! Always make sure that a back-up computer and projector pad are available. Better yet, bring along a back-up set of transparencies!

Flip charts

Flip charts are ideal for small audiences—departmental meetings or client presentations. They can be easily created by photographically enlarging overheads produced with a laser printer or high-resolution Linotronic phototypesetter. Flip charts permit close audience involvement. They can be viewed with normal room lighting. You can maintain close eye contact with your audience as you proceed through the presentation and pace your presentation on the basis of audience reactions.

The disadvantage of flip charts involves the time it takes to enlarge and mount them after you have created the slides. In addition, the size of the audience is limited to those who can sit around a conference table. Legibility usually drops off quickly as audience/presenter distance increases.

Use the questions in the following Presentation Planner as a guide to choosing the proper presentation media. You may want to make a copy of this worksheet and fill out a new sheet every time you begin a new presentation.

PRESENTATION PLANNER #1

1) *How long is my presentation supposed to last?*

   _____

2) *How many people are likely to attend?*

   _____

3) *How much eye contact and audience participation do I desire?*

   _____

4) *How much control over room lighting will I have?*

   _____

5) *How much time do I have to prepare the visuals for my presentation?*

   _____

6) *Do I have the tools needed to produce color slides or overheads?*

   _____

7) *Is airline travel involved in getting to the presentation?*

   _____

8) *If I am preparing a computer-based presentation, will a back-up computer be available?*

   _____

Use this worksheet as a guide for choosing the right presentation format.

Setting up your presentation

Once you have decided on the presentation format best-suited for your particular presentation needs, you can begin creating your presentation.

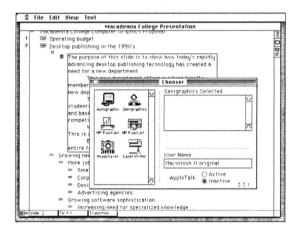

Choosing the right output device is the first step to a successful presentation.

If you are becoming involved with Persuasion from a background in word processing or desktop publishing, you may be surprised to find that the Chooser plays a very important role in Persuasion.

Previously, you may have printed most of your work on an Apple LaserWriter II NT or equivalent. Thus, you rarely needed to use the Chooser. With Persuasion, however, you are likely to use a wider selection of output devices. Indeed, it is likely that you may use more than one output device preparing a particular presentation.

- You may use your laser printer to print speaker's notes and audience handouts.

- You may use a color ink-jet printer to prepare overheads.

- You may send files to an outside service bureau, like Autographix or Genigraphics to prepare color slides and overheads.

Each choice changes the size and shape of the image you're creating. Thus, it's extremely important that you get in the habit of checking the Chooser, found under the Apple icon at the top of your screen, whenever you start a project.

HELPFUL HINT

Never begin working on a project without making sure that you have selected the appropriate output device with the Apple Chooser. Otherwise, you might have to go back and reformat each slide or overhead before it can be printed.

Next, load Persuasion by double-clicking on the Persuasion program icon.

When the Persuasion start-up screen appears, you can create a presentation based on a previously-prepared Persuasion AutoTemplate by clicking on "Open" and then double-clicking on the "AutoTemplates" folder and double-clicking on the name of an AutoTemplate file.

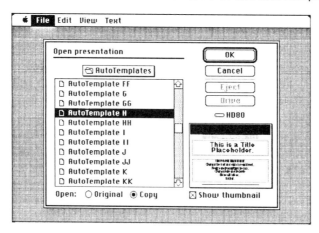

Persuasion 2.0 allows you to preview Slide masters before opening presentation files.

Note that as you click on the title of each AutoTemplate or stored previously-saved files, a thumbnail, or small reproduction of its Slide master, appears in a window at the right of your screen. If you're using a Macintosh II with a color monitor and the presentation was saved in color, the thumbnail will be in color.

In this case, however, click on "New" under the File menu. You will be brought to Persuasion's Outline view, with "Untitled 1" at the top of the screen.

Before proceeding further, however, click on "Page Setup" under Persuasion's File menu.

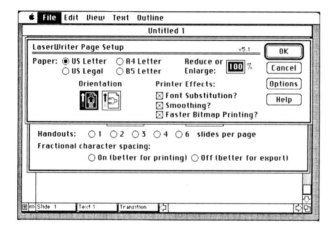

Page Setup screen

The first screen is the "Page Setup" screen determined by your previous Chooser choice. If you're using a LaserWriter, for example, you'll want to choose the paper size used. This option also allows you to specify the orientation and paper size used to print notes and handouts.

- Choose sizes over 100% if you are preparing flip-charts. (Large pages will automatically be tiled— printed on more than one sheet of paper.)

- "Orientation" lets you choose whether outline and handout pages will be taller than they are wide, or wider than they are tall. (Note: this only influences outlines and handouts—you must change slide or overhead orientation in the Slide master view, as described below.)

In most cases, you can safely leave the "Printer Effects" defaults as they appear.

- If you click on "Font Substitution," the LaserWriter will substitute Times Roman for New York and Helvetica for Geneva, if you forgot to format your outline, for example.

- Clicking on "Smoothing" can improve the appearance of bit-mapped graphics, such as imported graphic images prepared with paint-type programs.

- Clicking on "Faster Bitmap Printing" can speed-up printing, although some documents will not print.

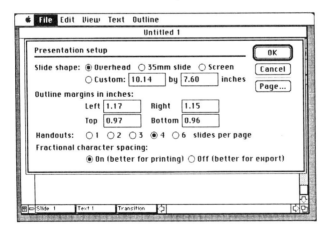

Presentation setup box

Next, click on "OK." The "Presentation setup" dialog box appears. This is where you format your presentation for either overheads, 35mm slides or computer-based, on-screen delivery. You can also change the margins around your slides as well as indicate the number of slides which will appear at reduced size on each page of your handouts.

Notice that default margins automatically change as you change the image area of your presentation.

If you indicate a page size larger than your LaserWriter paper size, a warning box indicates that the image will be tiled when printed.

Clicking "OK" twice returns you to Persuasion's Outline view.

HELPFUL HINT

When you click on "Overhead," the default measurements are 10.14 by 7.60 inches. This may, or may not, be appropriate for the overhead projector you will be using. Be especially careful when working with horizontal overheads. In many cases, you will want to choose a smaller dimension so that the overhead is centered at the upper part of the screen.

Slide orientation

After specifying the dimensions of your slides or overheads, you must specify their orientation. Click on "Slide master" under Persuasion's View menu. Notice that a Master menu now appears at the top of the page.

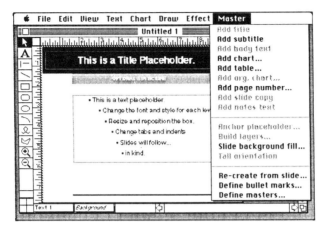

Master menu

Click on "Tall" if you desire vertical overheads and slides. Click on "Wide" if you want horizontal overheads and slides. After making your choice, you will be returned to Persuasion's Outline view.

HELPFUL HINT

If you are working with a previously-prepared AutoTemplate, remember that text and graphics on the AutoTemplate are not automatically reformated when you change slide orientation. Whenever you change slide orientation, you must reformat your Slide masters to accommodate the new orientation.

Step Two: Organizing and editing your ideas

After you've chosen the media most appropriate for your presentation and choosing the setup most appropriate for your presentation and loaded Persuasion, you can begin working on your presentation.

To get a better understanding of how Persuasion works, you might want to compare how working with Aldus Persuasion compares with traditional methods of presentation preparation. This will provide you with a perspective which will allow you to better appreciate how Persuasion works.

As you begin working on your presentation, one of two possible scenarios might be occurring.

- You might be worried that you don't have enough material to fill the time available.

- You might be overwhelmed by all the information you'd like to present and concerned that you'll never get it organized.

In either case, the stress caused by an inability to either get started or get organized makes your task infinitely more difficult.

Traditional presentation preparation

One of the reasons presentation preparation has always been so difficult and stressful in the past is the lack of a starting point and the lack of an easy way to organize your material.

Traditional presentation preparation is usually characterized as the "speech" approach. You sit down with yellow pad—or blank computer screen—and simultaneously try to write a speech like you'd write an article (or a novel). Unfortunately, you tend to end up trying to do too many things at once. You simultaneously try to add new ideas, edit existing words, reorganize ideas as well as worry about the appearance of your slides and overheads. The stress caused by this "task and information overload" is likely to result in procrastination and deadline madness. As a result, in many cases, neither speech nor visuals get produced.

What usually happens...

Working in this manner often results in a presentation which is "part speech/part visuals." Not only do you work slower than otherwise—because you're trying to do two things at once—but you often write your speech and then try to graft visuals onto it. The result is unnecessary effort plus a lack of coherence between words and visuals.

You not only have the stress of trying to write a speech, but you also have to retype your words when it comes time to prepare the visuals.

This approach usually results in a "stop and go" presentation style. As you deliver your presentation you tend to read a few paragraphs from the speech in front of you, look up, change your voice inflections, and then say: "As the slide indicates..." and then continue reading.

This type of presentation rarely proceeds smoothly. For one thing, you tend to become bogged down in details. You tend to spend too much time choosing words, rather than organizing ideas (and letting the words come naturally).

In addition, after you have written your speech and prepared your visuals, you have to go back and prepare audience handouts. You also have to reinforce your speech with visuals which will help you with your delivery. Your painstakingly-written speech has to be "reverse engineered" onto file-cards or a large-print outline which can be read at a distance.

Audience expectations

Compounding the problems described above is the fact that your audience doesn't *want* a speech. Your audience would rather you talk to them on a one-to-one basis.

Conversations are characterized by spontaneity and enthusiasm. Words come out in a natural, rather than a contrived, tone. When you talk to someone, you may have an agenda you're following, but you don't know exactly what every word is going to be until it's said. In short, speeches tend to be stiff and formal conversations tend to be informal and animated.

Worse, if you're delivering a "speech" and are interrupted by a question or comment, you can easily lose your momentum—and possibly your place. But, if you are delivering a presentation based on key points highlighted in your notes, you'll be much better able to handle interruptions.

Introducing the Persuasion alternative

Most presentations begin in Persuasion's Outline view.

Persuasion's Outline view takes the stress out of presentations, helps you organize your thoughts as well as simultaneously prepare visuals, audience handouts and presentation notes. Persuasion's Outline view thus provides you with the structure and clues you need to deliver an enthusiastic "conversation" with your audience.

While in Persuasion's Outline view, you can enter your ideas as quickly as they occur to you. After they have been entered on the screen, you can easily edit and reorganize these ideas.

Persuasion's Outline view:

- Helps you get ideas out of your mind and into the computer as quickly as possible.
- Makes it easy to edit and reorganize your ideas.

- Eliminates the need to be concerned with appearance and frees you to concentrate on content.

- Makes it easy to prepare notes and handouts as you organize your ideas.

The following section describes how Persuasion's Outline view operates. After we have seen the various options available, we can begin using the tools to create a sample presentation.

Working in Persuasion's Outline view

The first line you enter for each slide appears as the first slide title. Like all other slide titles, this should be a short, powerful statement which summarizes the information which appears below as subheads.

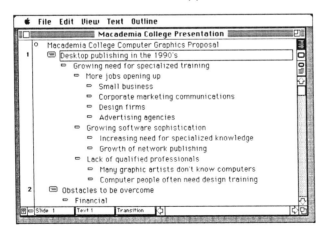

While you're entering text in Persuasion's Outline view...

Each of the subheads that follow should provide details that support the title. Persuasion's Outline view allows you to include up to six levels of subheads.

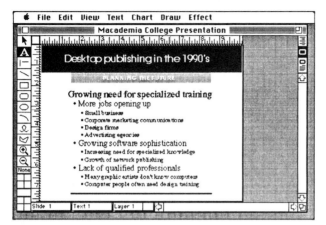

...the text is being formatted in the background, as you can see by changing to Slide view.

As described in Chapter Four, each subhead level can be individually formatted with a different typeface, type size and type style choice.

Central to the way Persuasion operates is the way unformatted text entered in Persuasion's Outline view is linked to formatted text which appears in Slide view as well as finished slides and overheads. Changes made in the Outline view are immediately reflected in Slide view—and changes made in the Slide view are automatically reflected in Outline view.

HELPFUL HINT

When working with the Apple Extended keyboard, remember the difference between the Return and Enter keys. The Return key enters a "hard" carriage return. It can be used to make one line of a subhead shorter than the lines that follow. The Enter key, however, inserts a new slide after the slide you're currently working on.

Entering slide titles

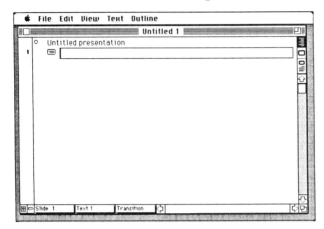

Even the most sophisticated presentation begins with an empty outline.

This is how most presentations begin. Start by typing in the first thought that comes to mind. Then hit Enter/Return. Notice that you are now one line lower but at the same indent level. Notice, also, that a new Slide icon has been added next to the line you have typed, and that a small number 1 appears next to the entry. Enter a few more lines, hitting Enter/Return after typing each line.

Entering subheads

Now, let's add subheads to each of the slide titles. Each subhead level should provide details which support the statement made at the previous subhead level. Avoid the temptation to introduce new ideas at the subhead level.

Starting by selecting a slide title by clicking on it. Hit Return and Tab. Type a new line. Hit Enter/Return.

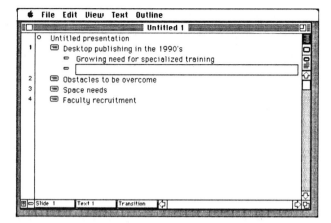

Screen shot

Notice that you are now at the same level as the previous entry. Type another line and Enter/Return. Once again, you are at the same level.

Changing the level of an idea

Sometimes you may want to promote or demote a subhead. In reviewing your outline, you may find that you have created a slide title that should really be a subhead of the preceding slide. Or, you may wish to convert a subhead into a slide title. Persuasion offers you two ways to change the levels of an idea.

To move a subhead to the left, making it more important, select it by clicking on it and:

- Select "Move left" under the Text menu.
- Use the Delete key.

To move a subhead to the right, making it less important, select it by clicking on it and:

- Select "Move right" under the Text menu.
- Use the Tab key.

As you can see, Persuasion's Outline view makes it easy to get ideas out of your mind and onto the screen of your computer where they can be easily prioritized. Persuasion makes it easy to establish the relative importance of ideas.

HELPFUL HINT

As you develop your outline, avoid subheads which introduce new ideas. New ideas should be slide titles rather than subheads. The only exceptions are "Summary" slides which provide a preview of slides to follow.

Editing copy

You can easily add, delete or change words as you prepare your outline. Editing can be done using your mouse or the Left/Right, Up/Down cursor control keys.

- You can use your mouse to move directly to the word you want to replace. Simply select the word by double-clicking on it. While it is highlighted, (the word appears as white type against a black background), you can type in a replacement word.

- You can select one, or more, words by clicking on the first letter and dragging the cursor through the words you want to replace.

- You can also use your cursor control keys to move around the outline.

Persuasion also makes it easy to delete or re-arrange word location.

To permanently delete a word, highlight it by double-clicking on it and either:

- Choose "Clear" under the Edit menu.
- Use your Backspace/Delete key.

To move a word to a different location, start by double-clicking on it. First:

- Choose "Cut" under the Edit menu.
- Execute the keyboard shortcut Command X.

Then, using the mouse or the Left/Right, Up/Down keyboard cursor control keys, move the cursor to the point where you want to relocate the word and either:

- Choose "Paste" under the Edit menu
- Execute the keyboard shortcut Command V.

The same techniques can be used to either delete or re-locate phrases. Simply highlight a word, phrase or sentence by dragging the cursor through it while holding the mouse button down.

HELPFUL HINT

As you edit your slides, avoid the temptation of including too much information. Slides and overheads should assist you, not replace you! Avoid including so much information that your audience spends all their time reading instead of listening. Use your slides simply to reinforce and organize your words.

Reorganizing your outline

You can also easily rearrange the order of your slides in Persuasion's Outline view.

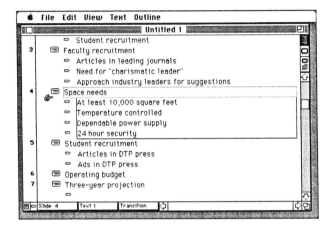

Choosing an Outline topic for movement.

Start by selecting the slide by clicking on the slide icon and hold down the mouse button. Notice that a small hand appears when you have selected a slide. After it has been selected, move the slide to its desired location. Notice how the hand turns into a horizontal bar at locations where it can be inserted.

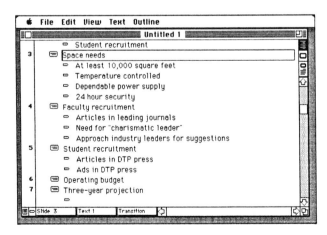

Repositioned topic.

Release the mouse button. This inserts the slide and re-numbers all the slides that follow.

The same technique is used to rearrange subheads.

Simply select the subhead by clicking on it and hold down the mouse button as you move the subhead to a new location within that slide or relocate it to a different slide.

Persuasion Version 2.0, (and following), allows you to simultaneously move more than one heading, or subhead, at a time. You can easily select two, or more, non-adjacent outline topics, or subheads, and move them as a group to a third location.

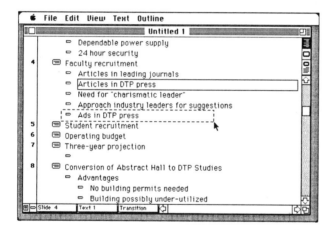

Using a marquis box to choose more than one subhead.

Start by holding down the Shift key by using your mouse to create a marquis box, or flashing dashed-line box, around the first outline heading which you want to move. Release the mouse button, but not the Shift key, when your first heading has been captured. Note that thick vertical lines appear in front of each captured line.

Still holding down the Shift key, use the Up/Down arrows, or high-speed elevator box along the right side of the outline to locate other sections of the outline you want to move.

Again, capture each desired heading, or subhead, by creating a marquis box around it using the mouse.

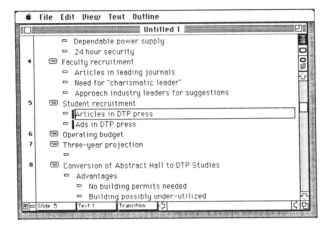

Multiple headings moved to a new location.

After all desired heads and subheads have been captured, as indicated by the vertical lines, click on one of the headings and drag the selection to its new location. The originally non-adjacent headings will appear together in a new outline location.

Alternately, using the same technique, you could delete the selection or move it as a unit to another presentation.

Moving around Persuasion's outline

There are two ways you can move from slide to slide.

- You can click on the slide icon you want to move to.

- You can use the Command key in conjunction with the Up/Down cursor control keys. The Up arrow returns you to the previous slide heading, the Down arrow advances you to the next slide heading.

HELPFUL HINT

You'll find yourself working much faster once you become familiar with Persuasion's keyboard shortcuts, like the use of the Command key in conjunction with the cursor control keys.

Creating new slides

You can convert a subhead into a new slide by selecting a subhead and choosing "Move Left" under the Text menu, or using the keyboard shortcut Command L.

As you become more comfortable with the various capabilities associated with Persuasion's Outline view, remember that the tools exist to make it easy to edit and reorganize your ideas. As you edit and reorganize your work, use the following Presentation Planner to keep you on track. Your answers to the following questions will help you take maximum advantage from Persuasion's editing power. Like the previous Planner, you might want to make copies of the following list on your office copier and fill out a new one each time you begin work on a new presentation.

PRESENTATION PLANNER #2

1) What is the single most important idea you want to communicate?

   _____

2) What is the next most important idea?

   _____

3) What action do you want your audience to take?

   _____

4) What evidence can you present to reinforce your arguments? ("Evidence" can be words, charts, graphs, illustrations or tables.)

   _____

5) What are the reasons your audience might not want to take the action you want them to take?

   _____

6) What evidence can you present to overcome these potential objections?

   _____

Use this worksheet to keep your presentation focused on your audience's needs.

Collapsing an outline

As you work on your outline, it will occasionally get so large that you cannot see all of the entries on a screen. When this happens, you can collapse the outline so that only the slide titles appear. This makes it easy for you to observe the overall development of your presentation. When viewing a collapsed outline, you can see at a glance if a supporting point has inadvertently been over-emphasized or an important point has been omitted.

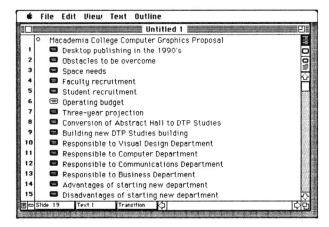

Collapsed outline

While outlines are collapsed, notice that the slide icons will be filled in, i.e. appear dark, if the slide contains subheads.

There are three ways you can collapse an outline.

- If you want to collapse all of the subheads throughout a presentation, click on "Collapse all" under the Outline menu.

- If you want to collapse only the subheads for a particular slide, click on the slide title and choose "Collapse subheads" under the Outline menu.

- You can collapse various levels of subheads by clicking on a subhead you want to remain, and choosing "Collapse subheads." This collapses just those subhead levels below the level you have chosen.

HELPFUL HINT

You can avoid removing your hands from the keyboard and reaching for the mouse by using the Command K keyboard command shortcut.

Expanding an outline

After an outline has been collapsed, you can expand it by clicking on "Expand all" under the File menu.

You can expand just one slide by first clicking on the title of the slide and then clicking on "Expand subheads" under the File menu or by using the keyboard shortcut Command E. This allows you to observe how the contents of an individual slide will fit in with the development of ideas which precede and follow it.

HELPFUL HINT

You can also collapse or expand individual slides by clicking on the Slide icon to the left of the slide title and then double-clicking. Double-clicking on a Slide icon in Outline view after it has been selected toggles between "Expand" and "Collapse" subhead views of that slide.

Deleting slides

At any time, you can return to the Outline view to delete unnecessary slides.

To delete a slide, click on the Slide icon at the left of the screen and click on "Clear" under the Edit menu.

When you do this, both text and associated graphics—like imported artwork or any charts or graphs you have created—will be deleted. This is not an irrevocable act, however. If you change your mind before you "Cut" or "Copy" any other text or graphics, you can restore the slide by either:

- Clicking on "Undo clear" under the Edit menu
- Using the Command Z keyboard shortcut

Importing previously-prepared outlines

Persuasion also allows you to import outlines created with programs like Acta or More. To import a previously-created outline, select "Import" under the File menu. Select the proper folder containing your outline file. Double-click on it, and the outline will appear in Persuasion format.

From this point, you can edit and reorganize the various headings until the right information is being presented in the right sequence.

Links with Slide views

Persuasion makes it easy to see how your words are going to appear when formatted into slides and overheads. Persuasion makes it easy to switch between Outline and Slide views. Slide views focus upon individual slides. Persuasion offers you four ways to switch between presentation views:

- While in the outline view, choose "Slide #" under the View menu. (In actuality, the "#" will be replaced by the number of the slide which your currently working on in the Outline view.)

- Simply click on the number of the slide in the outline view, to the left of the vertical line. This immediately takes you to Slide view.

- You can toggle between Outline, Slide and Notes view by holding down the Command key and using the Left or Right keyboard cursor control keys.

- You can go directly to Slide, Outline or Notes views by clicking on the appropriate icons located at the upper right hand side of your screen.

It's important to remember, however, that Persuasion's Outline view provides the basis of all presentations. This is because changes in the outline are automatically reflected in Slide views. (Likewise, additions, deletions or editing which takes place in the Slide view is automatically reflected in the Outline.)

The virtue of this scheme is that, as you outline your presentation, you're simultaneously entering text for individual slides and overheads.

Preparing speaker's notes

You can easily prepare notes to accompany your presentation. Notes consist of individual sheets of paper containing reduced-sized versions of your slides and overheads. These notes will "follow" the slides. Thus, if you re-arrange the order of your slides, the notes will also be re-arranged.

The notes you prepare should be simple elaborations or interpretations of the slide titles and subheads you're entering in Outline view. Using numbered or bulleted sentences or paragraphs, you can remind yourself of additional facts or anecdotes you want to communicate to your audience to support your on-screen presentation. For example, "Tell them what happened in Indianapolis!" You could also list the sources used to prepare your data, or present additional facts.

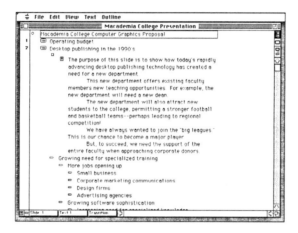

The Notes icon, which resembles an Apple Macintosh SE, indicates that what follows appears on the speaker's notes

Persuasion makes it easy to prepare speaker's notes while working on your outline. To add notes,

- Select "Add notes" from the Outline menu.
- Or, use the Command M keyboard shortcut.

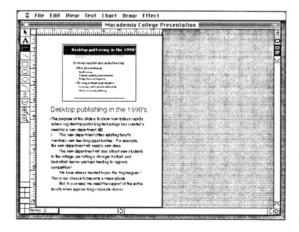

By clicking on the Notes icon at the right of your screen, you can view your notes at a variety of screen magnifications.

Notice that the "Notes" command acts as a word processor. Words automatically wrap at the ends of each line. You can use tabs and indents to visually isolate your thoughts. (In

Chapter Eight, we describe how to format your notes pages.)

When Outline notes have been hidden, a small diagonal icon appears in the extreme lower left of your screen. This is a reminder that notes have been hidden. You can immediately return the notes to the screen by clicking on this icon.

HELPFUL HINT

As you type your notes, each new paragraph is indicated by a new Notes icon. This allows you to easily reorganize your notes from the Outline view. To move a paragraph to a new location, simply select its Notes icon and move it to a new position.

Persuasion allows you to toggle between Outline views which alternately show or hide your notes. The ability to hide your notes is important, as it allows you to view, or print, your outline as a sequence of slides, without the notes interfering in the development of your ideas.

Select "Hide notes" from the Outline menu, or use the Command F keyboard command shortcut to toggle between Outline views with, and without, visible notes.

HELPFUL HINT

Avoid confusing "Hide notes" with "Remove notes." "Remove notes" is very similar to "Cut." If you inadvertently execute the "Remove notes" command, and change your mind, you must "Undo" your action before you perform any other action. Otherwise, the notes are permanently lost.

Persuasion Version 2.0's "Hide body copy" option allows you to create scripts for your presentation. These scripts contain just slide titles and notes. The "Hide body copy" option is available from the Outline menu, or you can access it through its Command B keyboard shortcut. When the "Hide body copy" option has been selected, a triangle appears beneath the slide number column at the lower left of your screen.

As you re-arrange your slides, the contents of the notes pages will automatically change. Thus, slides and notes will always be in synchronization.

Adding Subtitles

New to Version 2.0, (and following), is a feature which allows you to add subtitles to your outline. This subtitle is independent of the levels of subheads in your outline.

To add a subtitle to your outline, type it as if it were a subhead. Then, select it and open the "Set heading as" from the Outline menu and select "Subtitle." Alternately, you can use the Command 2 keyboard shortcut to create a subtitle out of any previously entered text.

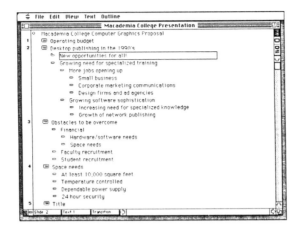

A small I-shaped icon visible in Outline view indicates that a subtitle has been added.

Notice that a small I-shaped icon indicates that the text has been designed as a subtitle.

HELPFUL HINT:

Subheads can be added to an Outline only if the Slide master you have created while formatting your presentation contains a subtitle placeholder. Space must previously have been designated on your Slide master for the subhead option to be available in Outline view.

Inadvertently making a subtitle out of a subhead confuses the status of the subheads subordinate to it. You will be presented with a series of question marks indicating the potential ambiguity. To solve this, select the subordinate subhead, or subheads, and execute the "Move left" command found in the Text menu. This restores the proper hierarchy to your outline.

Formatting outlines

Persuasion allows you to format all, or part, of your outline. This is especially important if you are using a LaserWriter printer. If you don't format your outline by choosing a LaserWriter typeface, it will appear in rather weak Geneva.

Persuasion makes it extremely easy to format your entire outline, or use a different typeface, type size and type style for each level.

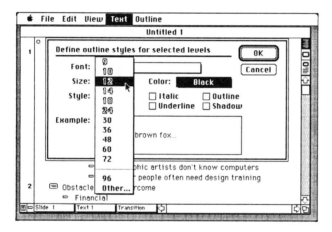

You can individually format each level of your outline.

Start by formatting the highest level of each slide's heading. Select the heading and select "Outline styles..." from the Text menu. This presents you with the "Outline styles" dialog box. Click on "Font" and you will be presented with a list of all available options. Select the typeface you desire and release the mouse button. Click on "Size" and scroll through the list of available options. After you have chosen the typeface and type size you desire, complete your formatting by choosing the type style you desire (Plain, Bold, Italic, etc.) Choose typeface color, if applicable. Notice that the options you have selected are displayed in the window.

When you have finished, click on "OK." Notice that every slide heading is now formatted the same way as the one you have chosen.

Next, select the next level of your outline and, again, select the "Outline styles..." from the Text menu. Again, choose the typeface, type size, style and color you desire for that level of your outline. Repeat this process until every level of your outline has been formatted.

HELPFUL HINT

If you want one or more, of all, levels of your Outline to share the same format, simply hold down the Shift key as you select each level of your Outline. Once again, a vertical black line will indicate that each subhead level has been selected. Select "Outline styles..." from the Text menu after all levels have been selected. Make appropriate typeface and type size decisions. Each level of your outline will now be identically formatted.

Note that Persuasion does not allow you to separately format subtitles. Subtitles share formatting with first level subheads. Notes, however, can be separately formatted.

Printing outlines

You can easily print an expanded or collapsed outline. Printed outlines are useful in that they allow you to easily review your work away from your computer. Printed outlines also permit you to prepare archive copies of your work. These copies make it easy to see your presentation as a whole, making it easy to review your work.

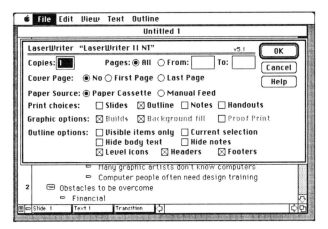

Before printing, make sure
you indicate which parts of
your presentation you want to
print.

To print an expanded outline, disable "Slides," "Notes" and
"Handouts" in the "Print" dialog box by clicking in the
boxes in the "Print" dialog box. Only "Outline" should
remain checked.

HELPFUL HINT

*It is extremely important that you get in the
habit of carefully checking Persuasion's "Print"
dialog box each time you print. For example,
you may only want to print your Outline while
you go out for lunch, but "Slides," "Notes" and
"Handouts" may be checked. At best, this will
only be an inconvenience. At worst, it could cost
a lot of unnecessary materials, if, for example, a
color printer was connected and you printed
your outline out on expensive color paper!*

To print a collapsed item, click on "Visible items only" in the
"Print" dialog box. A printed copy of a collapsed item allows
you to preview presentations too long to appear in their
entirety on the screen of your computer.

- The advantage of printing a collapsed outline is that it permits you to review the titles of your slides and overheads to make sure that important ideas are being introduced at the proper time.

- The advantage of printing an expanded outline is that you can double-check the contents of your entire presentation.

HELPFUL HINT

Always be sure that your screen is displaying the proper view of your outline before printing. Careful use of the various "Collapse" and "Expand" commands, as well as the "Hide notes" and "Hide body text" commands will allow you to print as much, or as little, of your outline as needed. For example, if you are going to distribute copies of your outline to the audience, you probably will want to make sure that speaker's notes have been hidden.

Exporting outlines

In addition to forming dynamic links with slides, notes and handouts, Persuasion outlines can also be exported to other formats. All, or just parts, of your outline can be exported. This can be a great time-saver to you if, for example, you should want to write an article based on your presentation at a later date.

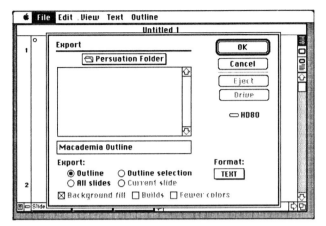

Screen shot—Export dialog box

To export an outline, click on "Export" found in the File menu. The "Export" dialog box offers you several alternatives.

- You can export your outline in text format, so it can be read by word processing programs.

- You can export your outline in outline format, as a More or Acta file.

- Slides can be exported as PICT files, so they can be enhanced by drawing programs like MacDraw.

- Slides can also be exported to the Scrapbook for use in PageMaker or other applications.

As you complete your first outline, you might want to ask yourself the questions in the following self-evaluation check-list. These questions can help you keep on track, ensuring coherence between the communications goals of your seminar and the development of your presentation.

OUTLINE CHECK-LIST

1) Except for "summary" slides which either preview upcoming slides or review previous slides, is each slide organized around one, and only one, major idea?

   _____

2) Does each slide use the minimum number of words needed to communicate the ideas it develops?

   _____

3) Have you avoided including any unnecessary information?

   _____

4) Have you avoided "buried subheads," i.e. introducing new thoughts at supporting, "detail" subhead levels?

   _____

5) Do your slides introduce information in a logical, orderly sequence?

   _____

6) Have you included "summary" slides which preview upcoming information and "review" slides which reinforce previous information?

   _____

Use this worksheet to review your completed outline.

Remember, the more time you spend planning and outlining your presentation, the less time you'll have to spend revising it!

Adding, deleting and moving among slides

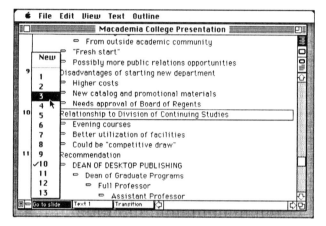

Persuasion's pop-up "Go to slide" menu allows you to go directly to new or existing slides.

In Persuasion's Outline view, a new slide is created every time you create a new outline heading. You can also create a new slide and go directly to it when working in either Persuasion's Outline or Slide views. Select the "Go to slide" pop-up menu at the lower left of your screen. This reveals a list of previously created slides.

- To go directly to a different slide, click on the desired slide number.
- To create a new slide, click on "New."

To delete slides, you must be in Persuasion's Outline view. While in Outline view, select the heading of the slide you want to delete and click on "Clear" under the Edit menu. This removes the slide and any associated graphics.

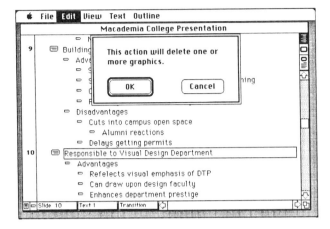

Verifying that you indeed want to delete a slide, along with associated graphics.

If graphics have been previously entered in Slide view, Persuasion will verify that you really want to delete the slide and associated graphics.

Persuasion's "Undo" command, at the top of the Edit menu, does, however, offer you an immediate opportunity to eliminate the deleted slide and restore the deleted graphic.

Review and looking forward...

By this point, you should have developed a strong outline of your presentation. Your presentation outline should contain a distinct beginning, middle, and end. There should be a mixture of slides which pace the development of your presentation and "detail" slides which focus on key, specific points.

In the next chapter, we'll examine how Persuasion's AutoTemplates and Slide masters work together creating a presentation. You'll learn how to create presentations based on existing AutoTemplates and create new AutoTemplates based on existing ones or built from scratch.

Chapter Three:
Formatting your presentation

Persuasion permits you to pre-define the size, placement and other attributes of words, charts and graphs as well as repeating visual elements like backgrounds, borders and your firm's logo. After you have established the desired format for your presentation, you can do most of your work in Outline view allowing Persuasion to automatically format your slides and overheads in the background. Here's how to base your presentation on one of Persuasion's thirty-six built-in AutoTemplates or create your own unique, formats and save them as AutoTemplates for later use.

"What are the tools you have to work with when designing a slide or overhead?"

As a preview of what's to come in the following chapters, let's take a brief look at the many design options you have for developing attractive, consistent, easy-to-read slides and overheads.

The easiest way to do this is to look at the options each of the primary building blocks of slide design offers you. Each of the building blocks of a slide or overhead can be broken down into numerous details which make it up.

As you review the summary below, you'll gain added respect for Persuasion's ability to let you specify these parameters in advance, so you don't have to constantly format them over and over again. After surveying the basic elements, we'll move on to Step Three: creating Slide masters for the various categories of slides you're likely to use in your presentation. The design of your presentation can be described in terms of:

Size and format

- Slide, overhead or on-screen presentation?
- Physical size
- Horizontal or vertical?

Background

- Color (or colors)
- Pattern

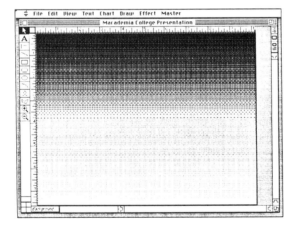

A slide background can consist of a smooth transition between two colors.

"Pattern" refers to whether or not the background will be a solid color, a textured effect created by the interplay between two colors (or black and white), or a smooth transition between a primary and a secondary color.

Borders

- Thickness
- Corner radius
- Color
- Pattern
- Shadow color
- Shadow pattern

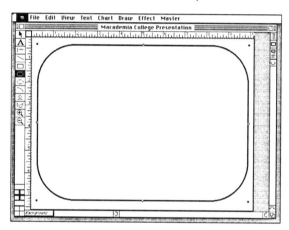

Creating a border with Persuasion's rounded corner box drawing tool.

There are two ways to create a border. One way is to simply use the line or box drawing tool to border your slide or overhead. As we'll see later, you can proportionately or disproportionately adjust the corner radius of the border to suit line thickness as well as the size of the box.

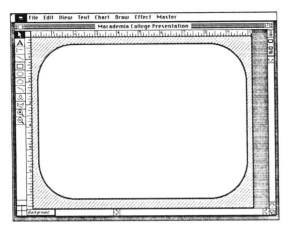

The diagonal lines—used for illustration purposes only—indicate how you can construct a frame, perhaps in a different color, around a slide.

Alternately, a border can be created by default. In this case, the border is created by the space between the edges of your slide and an inside box which creates the dominant visual for the slide.

Text

- Typeface
- Type size
- Type style (bold, italics, shadow, outline, etc.)
- Line length
- Line spacing
- Paragraph spacing
- Alignment (flush-left, centered, justified, flush-right)
- Tabs and indents
- Bullet size and type
- Color
- Shadow
- Background

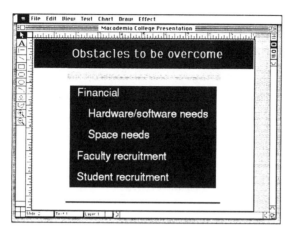

In this example, exaggerated for clarity, all three categories of text—title, subtitle and body copy—are placed in boxes which contrast with the slide background—which can be a different color.

Sometimes, text is emphasized by placing it against a background box. The color and pattern of this box should form a strong contrast against the slide background. This technique can also be used to emphasize charts and graphs or imported visuals.

Charts and graphs

- Type (pie, column, organization, etc.)
- Size
- Placement
- Colors
- Shadows
- Textures

Rules and boxes

- Color
- Thickness
- Pattern
- Line thickness
- Shadow color
- Shadow pattern
- Arrows or end caps

Identification

A final building block of presentation design consists of your firm's logo plus any other identifying information which is included on all slides. Information in this category could include:

- Presentation title
- The date of the presentation
- Audience or event name
- Presenter's name

The above are just a few of the many variables which, together, create repeatable formats for your slides and overheads. All of the above variables—and more—can be used to create Slide masters which will automatically format text which you enter into Persuasion's Outline view or charts and graphs which you either create using Persuasion's built-in charting and graphics capability or import from previously-created spreadsheets.

Design considerations

The way you handle each of the above options should be influenced by factors such as:

- Presentation media selected
- Room lighting
- Corporate design standards

The media selected in Step One should influence the design and format of your presentation. Slides offer the most sophisticated capabilities. Slides allow you far more color capabilities than color overheads. By choosing dark backgrounds, you can design slides which will allow the information to dramatically jump off the screen.

Black and white overheads are more limited. Screened backgrounds often appear mottled when used in overheads. For this reason, background and border treatments should be very restrained.

If you are going to be preparing an on-screen presentation, you'll want to be familiar with the capabilities of the monitors being used. Are color or black and white monitors available?

Room lighting

You have more creative opportunities available if you are going to present color slides in a dark room than a light room. Lighter background colors can be used in dark rooms than light rooms. As room illumination increases, lighter background colors stand a better chance of becoming washed-out.

Corporate design standards

Slides and overheads should never be created in a vacuum. Rather, they must conform to existing corporate design standards. These standards may be either formal or informal. Written standards usually specify:

- Logo size, color and placement
- Background and border colors
- Presentation identification information—date, occasion, etc.

Use the checklist below to help you begin making the appropriate design decisions for your presentation.

DESIGN GOALS CHECKLIST

1) What are the limitations imposed by the presentation media I will be using?

   _____

2) How bright is the room likely to be?

   _____

3) Does my presentation have to conform to any design standards?

   _____

4) What identifying information, if any, should be added to each slide?

   _____

Use this worksheet to make sure your design is compatible with the presentation media chosen, the presentation environment and existing design standards.

Step Three: Working with Persuasion's AutoTemplates

Aldus Persuasion offers you two ways to format your presentation:

- You can use one of the AutoTemplates included with Persuasion.

- You can easily create your own format, based on either an existing AutoTemplate or one you create from scratch.

In either case, after creating a unique format for your presentation, you can save it so it will serve as a template for later presentations you—or others—prepare.

Regardless how they're created, Persuasion's AutoTemplates automatically provide the art direction necessary to convert your outline into finished overheads and slides. While you're concentrating on content, Persuasion will automatically be adding the graphic touches necessary for appearance and consistency.

Multiple Slide masters

Consistency does not mean boredom, however. Each presentation template can include multiple Slide masters. These are accessed through the Master pop-up menu located second from the left at the bottom of your screen. This menu permits you to establish templates for various categories of slides. These categories might include:

- Title slide

- Slide containing a single, wide column of text

- Slide containing a two narrow columns of text

- Mixed slide—text plus visual

- Organization chart
- Chart or graph
- Concluding slide

At any point, of course, you might want to introduce even more variations. For example, if all of your slides are going to be text-oriented, you might occasionally introduce a different background color to help maintain the viewer's interest.

Previewing files

A new feature added to Persuasion Version 2.0, (and later), allows you to preview the Slide masters stored with AutoTemplates and previously-prepared files. This feature can save you a lot of time, as you'll be able to quickly "thumb through" your files until you find an Auto-Template or presentation which incorporates the particular "look" you're searching for.

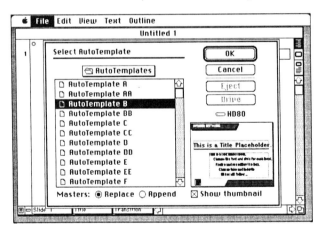

You can save time by previewing AutoTemplate files before they are opened. Thumbnails will appear in color when appropriate.

Working with an existing AutoTemplate

Let's create a sample presentation, based on one of Persuasion's AutoTemplates. These have been formatted for a variety of different overhead and slide presentations.

Start Persuasion, and click on "Open." Click on the "AutoTemplates" folder. Click You are then presented with an alphabetical list of template alternatives. Doubleclick on "AutoTemplate B."

Persuasion always starts in Outline view. To see what AutoTemplate B looks like, click on the Slide view icon at the upper right or open the View menu and click on "Slide 1."

HELPFUL HINT

Persuasion includes several keyboard shortcuts which help you navigate around the screen without using the mouse. For example, to move forward between Outline, Slide and Notes views, use the Apple, (or Command), key in conjunction with the Right keyboard cursor key. To move backwards between Outline, Slide and Notes views, use the Command key plus the Left keyboard cursor key.

You can easily preview each of the Slide masters associated with AutoTemplate B. Click on the second pull-up menu, "Title B" at the lower left of your screen. You are presented with a list of available Slide masters.

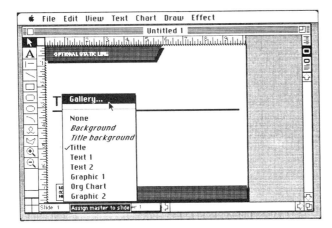

Slide master pop-up menu.

To see what they look like, click on "Gallery" at the top of the list. The "Set slide master" dialog box appears at the top of your screen, with a small preview box showing the currently-selected Slide master.

Click on the dialog box to the right of "Master" and you're presented with another list of Slide masters. Scroll through the list and click on each of the various Slide master alternatives presented. Each time you click, you can preview the Slide master associated with the name. This allows you to quickly scroll through your available options.

HELPFUL HINT

While in the Slide master view, you can preview previously-created Slide masters by holding down the Command key and using the Up and Down cursor arrow keys. This permits you to rapidly scroll through your alternatives and see them full size on the screen of your computer.

Notice the family resemblance between each of the Slide masters. Each Slide master offers different placement alternatives for slide titles, body copy, graphs and organization charts, yet the alternatives share similar borders and logo position.

Placeholders

A great deal of Persuasion's power is based on its use of placeholders.

Most Slide masters contain borders, space for your firm's logo plus one or more placeholders. (The logo is usually omitted when a large graphic or chart appears on the slide.) These placeholders are designed to be replaced by the particular text or graphics which make-up each slide or overhead.

There are several categories of placeholders. These include:

- Title
- Subtitles
- Body text
- Chart
- Table
- Organizational chart

Each placeholder defines the location, size and attributes of the text or graphics which will replace it (as described in the itemized lists above). Thus, you can predefine the typeface, type size, type style, alignment and color of text to be used in the "Title" of each slide. You can also predetermine the type, size, location and color of chart or graphs to be created using Persuasion's built-in charting tools.

Persuasion's use of placeholders frees you from the details of formatting your presentation, so you can spend more time in Outline view, developing new ideas and re-arranging their order. (In the chapters to follow, we'll show how to format these placeholders.)

Working with Placeholders

To get a better understanding of how Persuasion uses placeholders, click on the "Text 1" Slide master.

HELPFUL HINT

You can go directly to the Slide master view by holding down the Option key while clicking on the Slide view icon at the upper right hand side of your screen. You can return to Outline, Slide or Notes views by using the Command key in conjunction with the Left or Right keyboard cursor controls.

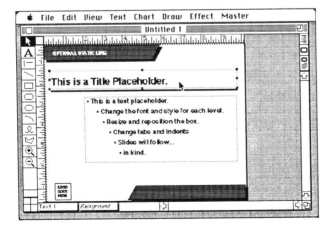

Selecting a title placeholder for formatting.

Click on "This is a Title Placeholder." Note that the line is now surrounded by eight dots. Click on the Text menu. By holding down the mouse button as you scroll down the list and moving your mouse slightly to the right as each of the available options are encountered (available options are highlighted in black, unusable options appear in light grey), you can see what formatting decisions have already been made and change those options.

For example, select "Font" to see which typeface has been chosen. Select "Size" to see what type size has been chosen. Likewise with "Style" and "Color."

To see how easy it is to change these formatting options in Slide master view, select "Alignment." Notice that "Align left" is highlighted. Scroll down the list of alignment options and click on "Align center." Release the mouse button.

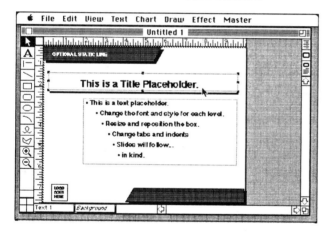

Title placeholder after choosing centered alignment.

Return to the Slide view, by either:

- Clicking on the Slide view icon at the upper right hand side of the screen
- Clicking on "Slide 1" under the View menu

Now, change to the outline view. Replace "Title" with "A New Title is Born!" To see how the formatting has been changed, change to the Slide view by clicking on the Slide view icon or clicking on "Slide 1" under the View menu. Notice that "A New Title Is Born!" is now centered.

HELPFUL HINT

When working in Outline view, you can go directly to the Slide view of any desired slide by clicking on the number of the slide at the extreme left hand side of your screen.

Replacing a placeholder

To see how Persuasion allows you to include your firm's logo into each slide, again click on the "Text 1" Slide master. Notice the "LOGO GOES HERE" placeholder at the lower left.

Let's assume that your firm's logo has been either created with a drawing program like Aldus FreeHand or has been scanned and cleaned-up with FreeHand and that you want to replace "LOGO GOES HERE" with your firm's logo on each slide.

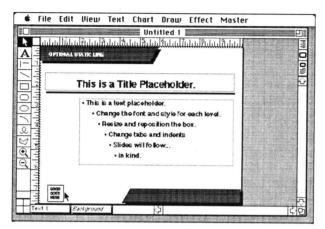

Selecting a logo placeholder so it can be replaced with your logo.

Advance to the Slide master view by clicking on "Slide master" under the View menu or holding down the Shift and Option keys as you click on the Slide view icon at the upper right of your screen.

Click on "LOGO GOES HERE" and Delete.

Open the File menu and click on "Import."

Click on the folder which contains the file with your logo. Double-click on the name of the file containing your logo.

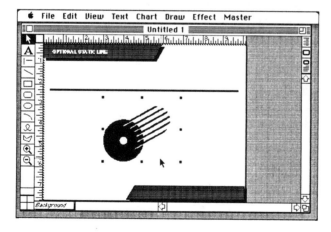

Importing a graphics file containing your association or firm's logo.

Your logo will appear in the center of your screen. Select it by clicking in the center of it.

HELPFUL HINT

Hold down the Option key as you click on the imported graphic in the center of your screen. This ensures that you will move the graphic, not the body copy placeholder.

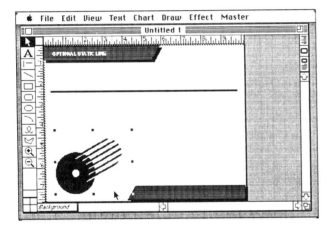

Moving the logo into place, before resizing it.

Place the imported logo at the lower left of the slide (where "LOGO GOES HERE" used to appear). Note that the imported logo is too large.

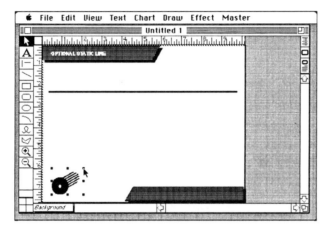

Holding down the Shift key while dragging maintains the aspect ratio—or height to width ratio—of an object as it is increased or decreased in size.

To enlarge or reduce your logo to proper size, hold down the Shift key while clicking on one of the four corner handles. Drag the corner handle until your logo is the proper size. After it has been properly sized, you may have to adjust the location of the logo until it's in exactly the right location.

After it has been properly sized, select it by clicking on it. Then copy it by clicking on "Copy" under the Edit menu.

Open another Slide master by clicking on one of the options in the pull-up menu box at the lower left of your screen. This time, click on the "LOGO GOES HERE" and get rid of it by clicking on "Clear" on the Edit menu or by using your Delete key.

Open the Edit menu and click on "Paste." Once again, the logo appears in the center of the screen. This time, however, you don't have to re-size it (unless necessary.) You can simply place it in the desired location.

In a similar way, you can add your logo to each of the Slide masters of your presentation. Using "Copy" and "Paste" saves time and ensures that the logo will always be the same size on each Slide master.

Working with a default AutoTemplate

If you had clicked on "New" instead of "Open," you would have been presented with Persuasion's default AutoTemplate, which is for an overhead presentation. This does not have to be your "permanent" AutoTemplate default, however. As described below, you can assign any AutoTemplate format to become the default format which is automatically opened (unless otherwise specified.)

Creating your own AutoTemplates

Start by holding down the Shift key while clicking on "New" under the File menu. This instructs Persuasion to ignore the default template—the template which is automatically chosen unless otherwise instructed. (If you find yourself always working with the same template, you can instruct Persuasion to automatically choose it upon start-up.)

HELPFUL HINT

Holding the Shift key down while clicking on "New" allows you to create a new presentation from scratch, ignoring any previously-saved default AutoTemplates.

Choose "Page setup" from the File menu, followed by "OK" in the "Page setup" dialog box. This brings you to the "Presentation setup" dialog box.

Notice that the default presentation is for overheads. If you are creating 35mm slides or an on-screen presentation, replace this default by clicking in the appropriate circle. In this case, in order to become acquainted with the way Persuasion handles colors, click on "35mm slide."

Next, choose "Save as..." from the File menu. Type an appropriate name for your template, i.e. "New Business Presentations."

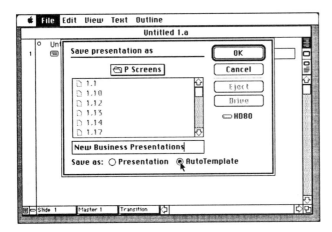

Files can be saved as either Presentations—which can be modified—or AutoTemplates—which can't.

Select "AutoTemplate" and click on "OK," (or hit Return). The reason for saving this file as an AutoTemplate is to preserve its integrity as you later create individual presentations based on it. You cannot over-write AutoTemplate files. This forces you to choose a new name each time you create and save a specific presentation. You're forced to give each future presentation a new name, i.e. "Intergalactic Motors Presentation," "Vern's Hobby Shop Presentation," etc.

Notice that "Master 1" appears in the pull-up menu at the lower left. If you click on it, and click on "Gallery," it will show up empty, indicating that no Slide masters have been saved.

To format your first Slide master, click on "Slide master" under the View menu. Or, to avoid removing your hands from the keyboard, click on the Slide icon at the upper right of the screen while holding down the Shift and Option keys.

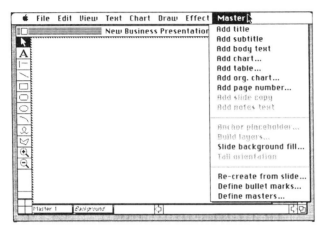

Choosing placeholders from the Master menu.

Notice that "Master" has been added to the menu bar at the top of the screen. Click on it. You will be presented with a menu of formatting options.

HELPFUL HINT

You can always quickly return to Slide master view by holding down the Shift and Option keys as you click on the Slide icon at the upper right hand edge of your screen.

Background colors

Start by choosing the background colors you'll want repeated throughout your presentation. Ideally, these colors should be based on both your firm's corporate colors as well as the format chosen for your presentation.

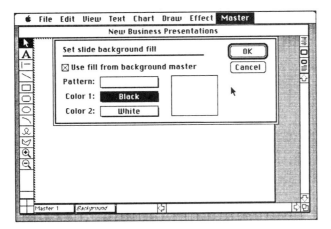

Choosing Slide master background colors and patterns.

Open the Master menu and click on "Slide background fill."

Start by picking the dominant background color. Start by clicking on the "Color 1" box.

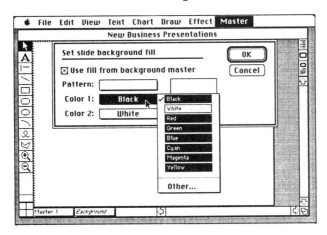

Choosing a primary color for a background, useful if you're working with a black and white monitor.

Your options are black, white , one of six basic colors, or "Other...."

REMINDER

Because black, white and six basic color choices are spelled-out on the color menu, Aldus Persuasion allows you to create color slides, even if you are working with a black and white monitor!

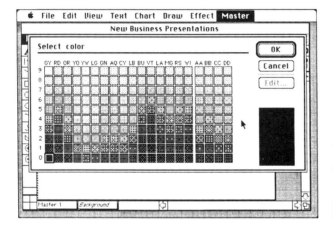

The "Select color" dialog box offers additional color choices. The large rectangle at right previews your choices.

If you click on "Other...," you are presented with a grid showing 144 pre-defined shades. Simply click on the appropriate box to select it. Notice that the large rectangle to the right of the screen changes color to reflect your choice. Click "OK" when you have chosen the primary background color you desire.

To the right is a second grid containing an additional 36 colors. These can be edited. If you are working on a Macintosh II and have a color monitor, click on one of them and the "Edit" option becomes available.

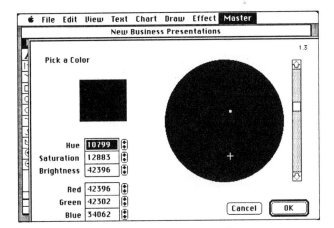

Viewed on a color monitor, or if this page was printed in color, the black circle in the "Pick a Color" box would be replaced by the full spectrum of available colors radiating from the center. Your choice would be previewed in the rectangle at left.

Click on "Edit" and you will be presented with the Apple Macintosh "Pick a Color" wheel. This fine-tunes your ability to choose precisely the color you want by offering you access to the full 16.8 million colors available on the Macintosh II.

Click on a point on the Apple Color Picker similar to the color you have previously chosen. Notice that the new color appears at the top of the rectangle on the left hand side of the screen while the original color appears below it. Use the elevator box along the right hand side of the screen to brighten or darken the new color. Experiment by clicking at various points in a straight line from the center of the circle to the edge. Notice how the color is purest at the edges and becomes weaker as you approach the center.

As you become more experienced working with color, you can "dial in" the precise mixture of hue, saturation and brightness, as well as red, green and blue to choose the precise color by number. Notice that these numbers automatically change as you use the Apple Color Picker. By making a written copy of the numbers which specify a particular color you have chosen, you can easily repeat your color choice at a later date.

Clicking on "OK" returns you to the "Set slide background" dialog box where you can choose a second background color, if desired. (Remember that just because a tool is available doesn't mean you have to use it!)

Background pattern

HELPFUL HINT

When choosing a two-color patterned background, Color 1 will be the darker color indicated in the pattern example, Color 2 will be the lighter color. If you are using the diagonal pattern, for example, Color 2 will be the dominant background color, while Color 1 will be the color of the diagonal lines.

Improving color quality

If you are working with a Macintosh II computer equipped with a color monitor, you can dramatically improve the way it reproduces background colors—especially patterns like shaded transitions between two background colors.

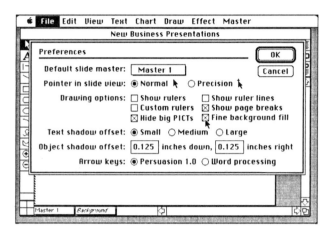

The "Preferences" menu allows you to customize your working environment.

To improve color quality, select "Preferences..." from the File menu and click on "Fine background fill." You will notice an immediate improvement in the way colors are reproduced in Slide view. Depending on your specific hardware, however, there may be a slight slow-down in performance, however, which is the reason "Fine background fill" is a selectable option rather than the normal default.

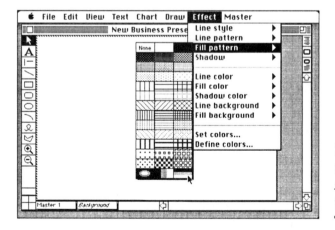

The bottom row of options in the "Pattern" box permits smooth transitions between two colors.

Next, click on the "Pattern" box. The pattern tool can be used to control how the two colors interact.

One option is to include smooth transitions from color to color. These transitions can take place from the center of your slide to the outside, or from top to bottom or left to right. Another option is to use a series of horizontal, vertical or diagonal lines. Notice, as you experiment with the various options available, you are able to preview your choice in the square box to the right of the pattern and color boxes.

Click "OK" when you are satisfied with your choices.

Creating a border

Next, create a border for your slides.

Click on the right-angle line drawing icon on the left hand side of the screen. Draw a line from the left to the right hand side of the screen. While the line is selected—indicated by the handles at each end—select "Line style" under the Effect menu.

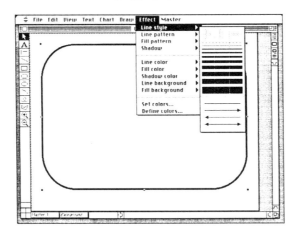

Modifying the thickness of the border surrounding a slide.

You can now select the thickness of the line. (The three squares at the top of the dialog box determine whether the option selected will change both vertical and horizontal lines, or just vertical or horizontal lines.) Scroll down and click on the fourth option down. As you release the mouse button, notice that the line becomes much thicker.

While the line is still selected, again open the "Effect" menu and select "Line color." Select "Red." Return to Slide view. If you are working with a color monitor, notice that the red line will be automatically added to each of the slides you create.

If you desire a squared or rounded-corner box around each slide, create one using the appropriate box drawing tool available along the left-hand side of your screen. After you have drawn the box, select "Line" from the Text menu to choose its thickness. While the box is still selected, choose "Line color" and choose an appropriate color for the box.

HELPFUL HINT

Careful use of the "Line" command under the Effect menu allows you to create a border thicker at the top and bottom than the sides, or vice versa. If you choose line thickness from the first column, under the + icon, the border will be equally thick on all four sides. However, if you select a thick line in the column under the horizontal line and re-select "Line" and choose a thin line under the vertical icon, there will be a gradual transition in the thickness of the border.

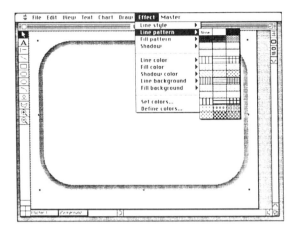

Choosing an appropriate line pattern.

In addition to selecting line width, you can select a desired pattern. If you have chosen a very thick line, for example, you could border your presentation with a variety of line patterns. While the box is selected, choose "Fill pattern." You are presented with a variety of options.

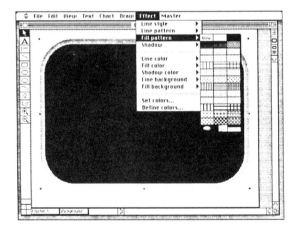

Choosing a fill pattern for the box—which can be a gradual transition between two colors.

While the box is selected, you can fill it with different patterns and colors—including transitions between two colors.

Helpful hint

A fill pattern of "None" allows boxes or circles to become transparent, allowing text or backgrounds to become visible.

Adding placeholders

After you have chosen the background colors and borders appropriate for your Slide master, you have to add placeholders for presentation text added in the Outline view. Placeholders also can be created for charts and graphs, organization charts and tables. You can also add a placeholder for numbers, so Persuasion will automatically number your slides or overheads—a big help if you drop your presentation on the way into the meeting room!

There are three types of text placeholders: titles, subtitles and body copy text.

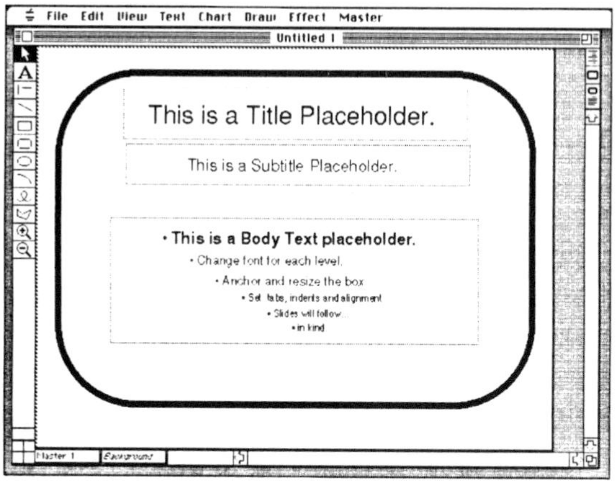

Slide master after title, subtitle and body text placeholders have been added.

Start by adding a title placeholder. Select "Add title" from the Master menu. Instantly, "This is a Title Placeholder." appears on the screen. Grab it and move it to an appropriate location on the slide.

Next, if you are using Version 2.0, (or later), select "Add subtitle" from the Master menu. "This is a Subtitle Placeholder" will appear on the screen. Move this into an appropriate location.

Then, select "Add body text" from the Master menu. When "This is a body text placeholder" appears, place it in an appropriate location.

Finally, choose "Add page number..." from the Master menu. When the box containing the twin X's appears on the slide, move it to an inconspicuous location.

Later, we'll add placeholders for charts and tables.

Adding a status line

Often, you'll want to add a status line to each slide or overhead. Status lines can be used to repeat the audience or presenter's name on each slide or overhead, or you can add the date of your presentation. To add a status line to your presentation, select the Text tool—the large A—near the top of the left-hand side of your screen and click on the desired slide location.

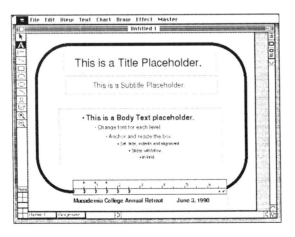

Adding a status line which will appear at the bottom of every slide.

Simply enter the text you want included on each slide or overhead. If the text appears too large or small, select the Text tool again and highlight the words by dragging the cursor across them. While they are highlighted, reformat the words using the various tools available under the Text menu:

- **Font**—allows you to select an appropriate typeface
- **Size**—allows you to choose an appropriate type size
- **Style**—choose between normal, bold, italics, bold-italics, shadow or outline
- **Color**—choose a color which contrasts with the background.

Text formatting will be covered in more detail in the next chapter.

Adding page numbers to slides and overheads

Page numbers are one of the most important types of placeholders you can add to Slide masters or Background masters. Page numbers help you keep your presentation in order—especially important in case you drop your overheads on the way into the presentation room! Page numbers added to Slide masters and Background masters are always correct. Persuasion automatically updates page numbers when you reorganize the sequence of your slides and overheads, as described in Chapter Eight.

Page numbers do not have to be large to be effective. Numbers can be formatted in small type, inconspicuously placed in the lower left corner of each slide. If you are adding borders to your slides and overheads, page numbers can be placed below or outside the lower border.

Adding page numbers is a two-step process:

- To add a page number, select "Add page number..." from Master menu. The "XX" page number symbol will appear in the lower center of your Slide master. Click on it and drag it to the desired location.

- Then, format it, by choosing the Text tool and dragging the I-beam through the XX's to highlight them, and then selecting the desired typeface and type size from the Text menu. (Text formatting is described in more detail in the next chapter.)

Page numbers are especially useful since Persuasion does not number audience handout pages—pages containing 1, 2, 3, 4, or 6 reduced-size versions of each slide or overhead. (Audience handouts are described in Chapter Nine.) These numbers will help keep your handout pages organized.

When printing handouts for an important presentation, after you have prepared the slides or overheads, you might consider opening the Slide or Background master and increasing the size of the page numbers so they will show up larger in the audience handouts. After you print the handouts, the page numbers can be returned to their original size.

Defining a Master

After you have created a Slide master to your satisfaction, it has to be given a name, so you can instantly choose it from among the other Slide masters you have created for other categories of slides. To do this, select "Define masters" from the Master menu.

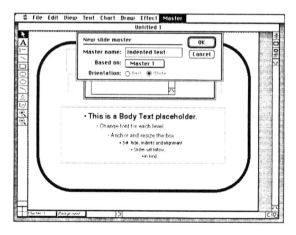

Naming a Slide master so you can easily recall it at a later date.

Type in the name you have chosen for the Slide master and click on "OK," or accept the name with your Enter/Return key.

By repeating the above process, you can define as many Slide masters as needed to accommodate the various categories of text and graphics likely to be included in your presentation.

Creating a Background master

As described above, Slide masters contain placeholders for titles, subtitles, body text and page numbers. With versions of Persuasion following 2.0, however, you can create a Background master which, itself, can be used as the basis for individual Slide masters. This Background master can contain a basic background color and pattern, consistent borders plus, for example, your firm's or association's logo.

This Background master can be used as the basis for creating individual Slide masters for specific purposes. By providing a consistent background, border and logo treatment, Background masters make it easier to create task-specific Slide masters, such as chart, text and title Slide masters. Background masters permit you to concentrate solely on positioning text and graphics placeholders for individual Slide masters. Background masters can save you a lot of time by allowing you to re-use basic background colors, borders and previously-placed logos.

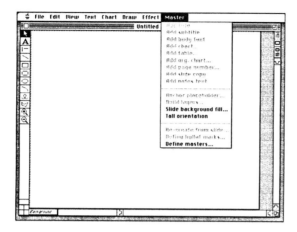

Fewer options are available when you select Background master.

To create a Background master, select "Slide master" from the View menu and choose "Background." Notice that the Master menu appears, but most of the entries are not available. The major option you can choose is the "Slide Background fill." Although you cannot add text or graphics placeholders, you can, however, use Persuasion's drawing tools to create borders and you can add status lines and import graphics—like your firm's logo.

After you have created a basic format for subsequent Slide masters, your presentation, return to the View menu and, again, select "Slide master."

Only, this time, select "Current."

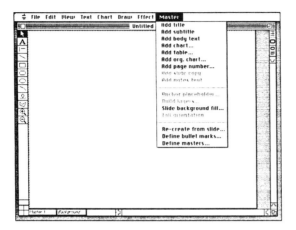

When you select Slide master—Current—more options become available.

This time, however, all of the Master menu options are available, including "Add title," "Add subtitle," "Add body copy," etc.

This time, however, when you open the "Select background fill" command, you will be prompted with a default which will ask if you want to automatically pick-up the underlying Background master's color scheme. You can, of course, if necessary, replace the default colors and patterns with new background colors and patterns.

To create additional Background masters, choose "Go to master" at the bottom of the View menu. Choose "New." Your new Background masters can be created from scratch, or can be based on elements copied from existing Background masters.

HELPFUL HINT

More than one Background master can be created for a given presentation. While in Slide master view, a listing of available Background masters can be seen by selecting the pop-up menu at the lower left of the screen. Background masters are indicated by italicized type, to separate them from Slide masters normally found in that location.

Creating Slide masters from existing slides

Another timesaver offered in Persuasion 2.0, (and later), allows you to create a Slide master based on a previously-created Slide master. Enter Slide view and create a new, blank master and select "Re-create from slide..."

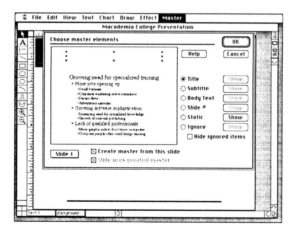

The "Choose master elements" dialog box allows you to choose which elements of an existing Slide master you want to include in a new Slide master.

Click on the Slide number pop-up menu and scroll through the list of available slides until you reach the slide you want to re-create. Click on "Create master" from this slide box, and click on the parts of the slide you want retained as placeholders in your new Slide master. Double-check your work by clicking on "Show."

Applying Slide masters

Aldus Persuasion offers you several different ways to apply Slide masters. You can apply or change Slide masters in Outline, Slide or Slide sorter views.

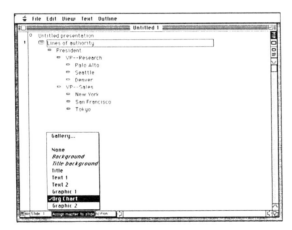

Choosing a Slide master from Outline view.

To observe this, close the presentation you have been working on, and again open AutoTemplate B to the Outline view. Notice that "Text 1" appears in the Slide master pop-up menu visible at the lower left of the screen. Click on the Slide master pop-up menu and select "Org Chart." Now, whatever you type in Outline view will be formatted according to the "Org Chart" Slide master.

To see this, change to the Slide view by one of the three options available:

- Clicking on the Slide view icon at the upper right of the screen
- Selecting "Slide 1" under the View menu
- Clicking on the slide number in bold at the left side of the Outline screen (in this case, "1")

If desired, you can again use the Slide master pop-up menu at the lower left of the screen to change the appearance of the slide.

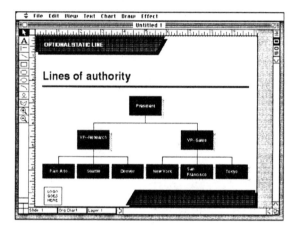

Outline text after it has been automatically formatted according to the Organization Chart Slide master.

You can also format slides in Persuasion's Slide sorter view.

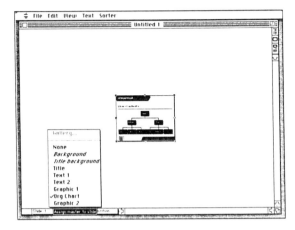

Slide masters can also be applied in the Slide view.

Persuasion's Slide sorter view fills your screen with miniature views of each of the slides you have created. You can apply a Slide master to one, or more, slides in the Slide sorter view. To illustrate how this operates, choose "Slide sorter" under the View menu. Since your outline is, presumably, empty, only one slide will be shown. Select this slide by clicking on it.

HELPFUL HINT

You can choose more than one slide for reformatting by holding down the Shift key as you click on additional slides.

While one or more slides have been selected, you can change their formatting by opening the Slide master pop-up menu at the lower left of the screen and choosing a different Slide master.

This ability to format slides in various views is just another of the features which makes Persuasion an exceptionally easy-to-use, very powerful tool.

Assembling Slide masters from existing presentations

Persuasion 2.0 allows you to create a presentation, or an AutoTemplate, which contains Slide masters included in one, or more, previously-created presentations or AutoTemplates. This can be a great time-saver, allowing you to base new presentations on previously-created work.

To import masters from an existing AutoTemplate or presentation, select the "AutoTemplates" command from the File menu.

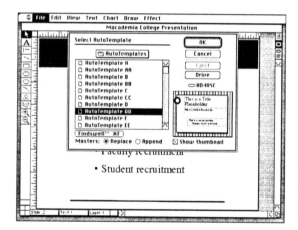

Using the "AutoTemplates" command, you can add AutoTemplates from a previously-created presentation to your current presentation.

Scroll through the list of previously-created AutoTemplates and presentations. Notice the "Show thumbnail" option which shows you a reduced-sized view of the presentations as you scroll through them.

When you come to the desired AutoTemplate or presentation, click on it. You must then decide whether you want to replace your current Slide masters or add them to your existing Slide masters.

- If you choose "Replace," all Slide masters will be replaced. If your existing presentation contained a Slide master with the same name as the incoming Slide master, the incoming Slide master will replace the existing one. Likewise, text, color and chart formats will replace those in the existing presentation.

- If you choose "Append," incoming Slide masters will be added to existing Slide masters. When identical names are encountered, the imported Slide master will be modified so it can be distinguished from the existing Slide Master. Likewise, incoming chart and text formats will be added to existing text formats. Existing colors will not be affected.

Saving your templates

There are three ways to save your work:

- As a Presentation
- As an AutoTemplate
- As a default AutoTemplate

It's always a good idea to immediately give your work a name and save it. This permits you to make incremental saves as you work. Remember that, until you save it, your work exists only in your computer's memory. Unless you have saved your work, a momentary power supply interruption can cause you to lose hours of work.

To save your work, click on "Save" under the File menu—or use the keyboard command shortcut Command S. You will be presented the "Save presentation as" dialog box.

Click on "Presentation" if your file is to be used for a specific presentation. After clicking on "Presentation," you might want to place the presentation in an appropriate "Client" or "New Business" folder.

Click "AutoTemplate" if you want to use the template as the basis of future presentations. Again, before you save your work, you might want to place the file in your AutoTemplates folder, or create a "Templates" or "New Business" folder.

HELPFUL HINT

Name and save your presentation or Autotemplate as soon as possible, and get in the habit of frequently saving your work. Aim to save your work every ten minutes, or so. This will minimize lost work, in case your computer's power supply is interrupted. In addition, if your presentation suddenly begins to veer off in a direction you're not comfortable with, you can return to the last saved version without losing too much work.

Creating a default AutoTemplate

To save your work as a default AutoTemplate which will be automatically activated when you open a "New" file, start by selecting "AutoTemplate" in the "Save presentation as" dialog box. Select your hard drive. Choose your System folder.

Give the AutoTemplate default file you're saving the title: "Persuasion Prefs". (Be sure you spell it exactly as shown). Click on "OK," (or press Enter/Return).

This will be the AutoTemplate automatically chosen the next time you open a new file.

HELPFUL HINT

When creating a default AutoTemplate, be sure that you carefully spell the "Persuasion Prefs" filename and that you place the file in your System folder.

CHECKLIST—REVIEWING SLIDE MASTERS

1) *Are your design decisions appropriate for the presentation media you have selected?*

    _____

2) *Do your design decisions take into account probable room lighting conditions?*

    _____

3) *Do your slides or overheads present a consistent appearance with each other?*

    _____

                                    (continued)

Use this checklist to make sure that your Slide masters are appropriate for your presentation.

4) Have you created enough Slide masters for all of the various categories of slides and overheads you're likely to use in your presentation?

_____

5) Is the design of your presentation compatible with existing corporate or association design standards?

_____

6) Did you exercise restraint and design for simplicity?

_____

7) Have you included repeating elements like logo and presentation identification information?

_____

8) Have you avoided mixing horizontal and vertical slides in the same presentation?

_____

9) Have you added page numbers and status lines to your Slide masters?

_____

10) Did you include sufficient contrast between the various elements of slide architecture?

_____

Slide master checklist, continued.

Review and looking forward...

By now, you have a good start on both the content and the basic appearance of your presentation. Having surveyed how Persuasion's Slide master and placeholder features work, in the chapters to come, we'll take a closer look at working with the various building blocks of slide and overhead design. We'll look in greater detail at adding and formatting text placeholders as well as adding various types of charts, graphs and tables to your presentation.

Chapter Four:
Adding, editing and formatting text

Although backgrounds, borders, charts and graphs create visual excitement, words form the backbone of your presentation. In this chapter, we look at how Persuasion helps you translate Outline view text into exciting high-impact, fully formatted words. This involves adding and formatting title, subhead and body text placeholders added to Slide masters. It also involves formatting text enhancements like backgrounds, bullets and shadows.

Step Four involves formatting the outline you prepared in the preceding chapter using Persuasion's many text formatting tools. These tools give you total control over the typeface, type size, type style, alignment and color of every category of text added in Persuasion's Outline view or typed directly on individual slides.

As we proceed through this chapter, you'll probably be surprised that so many formatting options are available. You'll probably also notice that we will be employing many of the techniques previously introduced—especially the tools used to select and manipulate color.

Because of the wealth of formatting options Persuasion offers you, this chapter is divided into two parts: basic and advanced.

Basic formatting options include:

- Choosing the right typeface, type size and style
- Adjusting line length and choosing the proper alignment
- Adjusting tabs and options

Advanced formatting options include:

- Text color, patterns and shadows
- Background colors, frames, and patterns
- Enhancements like bullets and shadows

After you have established how you want various categories of text to appear, you can save these choices as Formats which can be quickly and easily applied to any text. You can also check your spelling and use Persuasion's Search and Replace function to make any last-minute changes in your presentation.

Our tour through Persuasion starts by formatting the three major text placeholders added in the previous chapter to your Slide master:

- Titles
- Subtitles
- Body copy

HELPFUL HINT

You'll find clicking on a text block and directly applying formatting will save you a lot of time. When all of the text in a block is going to be formatted the same way, simply click on the block and proceed directly to the Text menu.

Selecting text for formatting

Regardless of the type of formatting you desire to apply, Persuasion offers you two ways to select the type:

- Using the arrow, or Selection tool, click anywhere within the invisible box which surrounds a text block. This selects the text—making the eight dots which surround the text block visible.

- You can be more selective by first choosing the Text tool, represented by the A-icon at the top left of your screen, and dragging the Text I-beam through the letters, sentences, or paragraphs you want to format. Hold down the mouse button as you highlight one, or more, lines of text. Highlighted lines will appear against a grey or colored background, depending on the type of monitor you're working with.

These techniques work in both Slide master and Slide views.

HELPFUL HINT

You will find clicking on a text block and applying desired formatting to be a great timesaver. When all the lines in the block are going to be formatted the same way, simply click on the text block and proceed directly to the Text menu.

Formatting existing AutoTemplates

If you have not already done so, start Persuasion. Click on "Open," double-click on the AutoTemplates folder and double-click on "AutoTemplate B." As usual, Persuasion opens to the Outline view.

Click on "Slide master" under the View menu. Then select "Current."

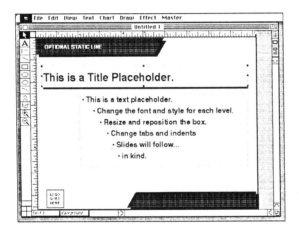

Clicking on the title placeholder is the first step in applying text attributes.

You will be presented with the default Text 1 Slide master. Click on "This is the Title Placeholder." Notice that eight dots now appear around the title. These are used to adjust line length as well as the title placeholder's position on the slide.

Choosing the right typeface

The first step in formatting text is to choose the right typeface. Click on the Text menu and choose "Font."

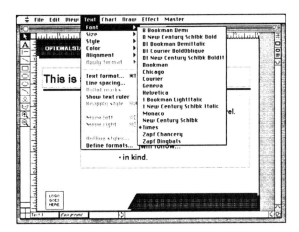

Selecting "Font" from the Text menu displays all available typeface options.

You will be presented with a list of available font options. Hold down the mouse button and scroll down the list until the typeface you want is highlighted. Release the mouse button and the desired typeface will be chosen.

Choose "Times" and release.

Helpful hint

Your choice of typefaces should be influenced by the output device you will be working with. Be sure that the typefaces you choose can be printed by the output device you will be working with. For example, Adobe PostScript typefaces will not print on QuickDraw printers or film recorders like the Presentation Technologies Montage Film Recorder.

Typeface characteristics

For the most part, your typeface alternatives are limited to the basic fonts available with the Apple LaserWriter II NT. These include:

- Three sans serif typefaces—Avant Garde, Helvetica and Helvetica Narrow

- Four serif faces—Bookman, New Century Schoolbook, Palatino and Times Roman

- One script—Zapf Chancery

- One set of decorative symbols—Zapf Dingbats

- Courier—a typewriter-like font

These typefaces are also supported by film service bureaus like Autographix and Genigraphics. Similar typefaces are also available for use with QuickDraw color printers like the Hewlett-Packard PaintJet and PaintJet XL.

HELPFUL HINT

By sticking with the basic typefaces described in this section, you will be able to create presentations which can be easily printed on more than one output device. For example, you'll be able to print black and white overheads on on your Apple LaserWriter II NT and, with only minor modifications, transmit the same presentation to an outside service bureau-- like Genigraphics—and have them prepare color slides based on the same typography.

You sacrifice this mobility when you create your presentation using typefaces incompatible with film recorders and outside service bureaus. If you use a non-standard typeface, you'll have to go through your presentation and reformat each overhead before preparing color slides!

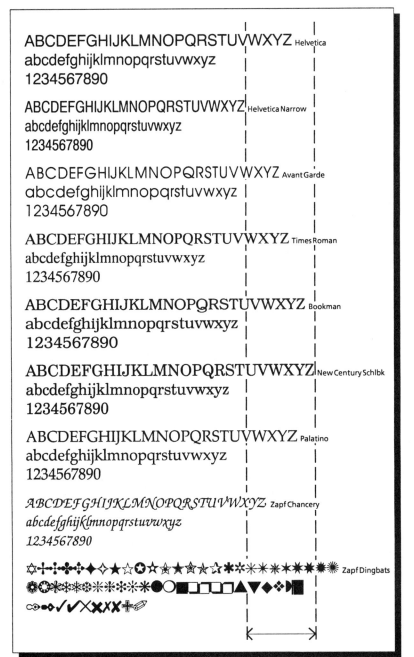

ABCDEFGHIJKLMNOPQRSTUVWXYZ Helvetica
abcdefghijklmnopqrstuvwxyz
1234567890

ABCDEFGHIJKLMNOPQRSTUVWXYZ Helvetica Narrow
abcdefghijklmnopqrstuvwxyz
1234567890

ABCDEFGHIJKLMNOPQRSTUVWXYZ Avant Garde
abcdefghijklmnopqrstuvwxyz
1234567890

ABCDEFGHIJKLMNOPQRSTUVWXYZ Times Roman
abcdefghijklmnopqrstuvwxyz
1234567890

ABCDEFGHIJKLMNOPQRSTUVWXYZ Bookman
abcdefghijklmnopqrstuvwxyz
1234567890

ABCDEFGHIJKLMNOPQRSTUVWXYZ New Century Schlbk
abcdefghijklmnopqrstuvwxyz
1234567890

ABCDEFGHIJKLMNOPQRSTUVWXYZ Palatino
abcdefghijklmnopqrstuvwxyz
1234567890

ABCDEFGHIJKLMNOPQRSTUVWXYZ Zapf Chancery
abcdefghijklmnopqrstuvwxyz
1234567890

Zapf Dingbats

The distance between the vertical lines illustrates the difference in line-length between the longest, (New Century Schoolbook), and shortest, (Helvetica Narrow), upper case alphabets.

Helvetica

ABCDEFGHIJKLMNOPQRSTUVWXYZ
abcedfghijklmnopqrstuvwxyz
1234567890

Helvetica is the basic sans serif typeface. Sans serif refers to the lack of feet, or tiny decorations, at the edges of each letter. Serifs add character to a typeface and provide letter-to-letter transitions which aid the reader. Helvetica's popularity is based on its straightforward legibility. Upper and lower case letters are clearly identified, even at long viewing distances. The letters are comfortably spaced.

Helvetica Narrow

ABCDEFGHIJKLMNOPQRSTUVWXYZ
abcedfghijklmnopqrstuvwxyz
1234567890

Helvetica Narrow is a special version of Helvitica that has been horizontally "condensed." It maintains the "family look" of Helvetica, but permits you to squeeze more words on each line. Helvetica Narrow is an excellent choice for status lines and call-out's.

Avant Garde

ABCDEFGHIJKLMNOPQRSTUVWXYZ
abcedfghijklmnopqrstuvwxyz
1234567890

Avant Garde is an alternative which should be used with more discretion. The shape of Avant Garde's letterforms are more rounded, which somewhat compromises legibility—or the ability to differentiate each letter. The lower case Avant Garde alphabet takes up more space than lower case Helvetica, yet, because of the similar shapes shared by so many of the letters, it's easier to mix up the letters. Notice, for example, how distinct the lower case Helvetica a, b, c, d, and appear, compared to the basically similar appearance of the lower case Avant Garde a, b, c, d, and e. Although Avant Garde's letters are wider than Helvetica's, letter spacing appears to be tighter, which also compromises legibility under certain circumstances.

Thus, although Avant Garde can project a more contemporary appearance, this has to be balanced against compromised legibility—especially at long viewing distances.

Times Roman

ABCDEFGHIJKLMNOPQRSTUVWXYZ
abcedfghijklmnopqrstuvwxyz
1234567890

Times Roman has long been considered the "basic" serif type face. Times Roman works especially well at large sizes. Although a very popular face, Times Roman occasionally has problems at small size. This is often due to stress—the difference in thickness between the horizontal and vertical strokes which make up each letter. Sometimes, the thin strokes almost disappear, especially at small sizes or long viewing distances, or if there is insufficient color contrast between Times Roman text and background colors.

Bookman

ABCDEFGHIJKLMNOPQRSTUVWXYZ
abcedfghijklmnopqrstuvwxyz
1234567890

Bookman is an excellent alternative to Times Roman. Bookman letters tend to be a bit fuller than Times Roman. This slightly cuts down on word density—the number of words which will fit on a line--but improves legibility. Stress is less of a problem. There is less chance that thin strokes will become "lost" on the screen.

New Century Schoolbook

ABCDEFGHIJKLMNOPQRSTUVWXYZ
abcedfghijklmnopqrstuvwxyz
1234567890

New Century Schoolbook is similar to Bookman, yet has a bit more "character" than either Times Roman or Bookman. Compare New Century Schoolbook's flamboyant upper case Q with the more restrained Times Roman Q. Notice that although the New Century Schoolbook upper case alphabet is longer than the Bookman upper case alphabet, the lower case alphabet is shorter.

Palatino

ABCDEFGHIJKLMNOPQRSTUVWXYZ
abcedfghijklmnopqrstuvwxyz
1234567890

Palatino should be used with discretion in presentations. Unless used at large size, Palatino's extreme stress and tiny serifs can easily get lost. Palatino can be effectively used at large sizes—perhaps in titles—to present a "classic" or "expensive" appearance.

Zapf Chancery

ABCDEFGHIJKLMNOPQRSTUVWXYZ
abcedfghijklmnopqrstuvwxyz
1234567890

Zapf Chancery is a distinctive script face, perhaps best reserved for slide titles or—perhaps—client or presenter status lines.

Zapf Dingbats

Zapf Dingbats is a collection of symbols which can be used to enliven your presentation. Zapf Dingbats consists of a variety of decorative symbols which can be used in bullet lists in place of asterisks or bullets. A variety of boxes, checkmarks, pointing hands, stars, triangles and plus signs are included to brighten your presentation.

Courier

```
ABCDEFGHIJKLMNOPQRSTUVWXYZ
abcedfghijklmnopqrstuvwxyz
1234567890
```

Choose Courier when you want your presentation to reflect a "last-minute/fast-breaking-news," informal or "typewritten" look. Courier forms a dramatic contrast to the more formal, or stylized, typefaces like Helvetica, Times Roman or Palatino.

In general, the simpler the typeface design, the better. Ornate typefaces tend to slow down readership—especially at long distances.

HELPFUL HINT

In many cases, good-looking slides and overheads can be created by contrasting sans serif slide titles and subtitles with serif subheads and body copy. Your slides and overheads can quickly become boring if only one typeface is used for titles, subtitles and body copy.

Additional typeface alternatives

Although many successful presentations are created using the basic LaserWriter faces, especially Times Roman and Helvetica, this doesn't mean you have to close your mind to additional alternatives. This is especially true if you are preparing:

- Black and white overheads for printing on a PostScript printer like the Apple LaserWriter II NT
- Color overheads for printing on a PostScript color printer like those made by QMS and Tektronix

In addition, your typeface capabilities are expanded if you are using the Adobe Type Manager and the Hewlett-Packard PaintJet or Paintjet XL color printers. Although the Hewlett-Packard PaintJets are not PostScript printers, when used with the Adobe Type Manager, they can faithfully reproduce all Adobe PostScript fonts.

HELPFUL HINT

The Adobe Type Manager should be considered a virtual necessity for any serious Persuasion user. The Adobe Type Manager dramatically improves the appearance and accuracy of typeface displays on the screen of your computer. It eliminates jagged outlines and permits you to do a better job of previewing the appearance of your slides. It also improves printing quality with printers like the Hewlett-Packard PaintJets and improves the appearance of on-screen Slide show presentations.

If you are searching for a more distinctive typeface repertoire, one excellent choice is the Adobe Presentation Package which consists of three typeface families which were chosen specifically for presentation use. The Adobe Presentation Package includes two serif and one sans serif typefaces which were chosen on the basis of their legibility. Because of their simple, straightforward design, the letterforms used in these typefaces can be easily read from a long distance.

Selecting the right type size

Next, choose the desired type size. While "This is the Title Placeholder" is still selected, open the Text menu, select "Size" and scroll down the list of available type sizes until you come to the desired type size. Outlined options will deliver the best on-screen displays. If you do not see a desired type size, click on "Other." This allows you to specify a point size option not listed as a default.

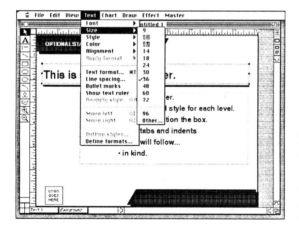

If you are sending your files to a service bureau for color slides or overheads, limit your typeface choices to the alternatives listed in the Size menu.

Remember that type is specified in points and picas. There are 72 points to an inch. Thus, thirty-six point type appears one-half inch high, eighteen point type is approximately one-quarter inch high.

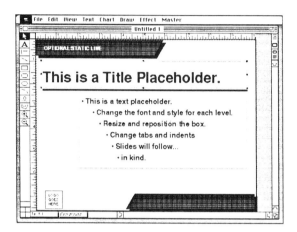

Title placeholder after reformatting.

Choose "48" and notice how the text is immediately reformatted.

You can use type size choices to add visual interest to your slides and overheads as well as make it easier for readers to identify the various levels of detail in your slides. Ideally, your title placeholder should be set in a significantly larger type size than the supporting information.

HELPFUL HINT

Be sure to install all sizes of the Persuasion screen fonts included with the software and only select type sizes which appear on the Persuasion menu. On-screen displays will be enhanced if the larger font sizes have been installed.

If you select in-between sizes, you may run into problems involving line-length if you later send your presentation to a service bureau. Lines which appear "just right" on the screen of your computer may turn out to be too long when an outside service bureau prepares 35mm slides.

Remember that the number of words which will fit on a line declines as you choose larger type. Larger type occupies more space than small type, hence fewer words will fit.

Change type style

While "This is a Title Placeholder" is highlighted, click on "Style" and observe the various options available. In general, your choices will be between "Plain," "Bold" and "Italic," although, as we shall see later, the "Shadow" and "Outline" options offer permits you to create additional distinctive effects.

Select "Bold" to give your slide titles a heavier look.

Persuasion 2.0, (and following), incorporates several important keyboard shortcuts which can speed your text formatting. These shortcuts help you avoid the need to open the Text menu, choose "Style" and select the type style desired. For example:

- **Plain**—hold down the Shift and Command keys and hit the spacebar.
- **Bold**—hold down the Shift and Command keys and type B.
- **Italic**—Hold down the Shift and Command keys and type I.
- **Underline**—Hold down the Shift and Command keys and type U.
- **Outline text**—Hold down the Shift and Command keys and type O.
- **Shadowed text**—Hold down the Shift and Command keys and type S.

Choosing line length

To reduce line-length, select the middle dot in the left-hand handles. Move it to the right. Then, select the middle dot on the right-hand side of the title placeholder. Move it to the left. You can use these handles to increase or decrease line length for all levels of text.

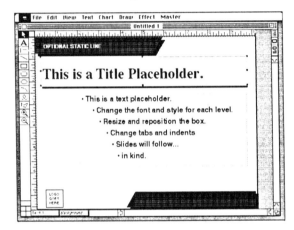

Line length can be adjusted by dragging the center dots on the left- and right-hand sides of the title placeholder.

When you shorten line length, notice how the title placeholder automatically wraps over two lines.

Moving a text placeholder

Notice that, when you decreased line length and caused the title placeholder to wrap over two lines, it now partially obscures the trapezoidal box which defines the top of the slide.

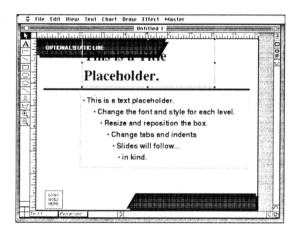

Reducing line length forces the title text to wrap over two lines.

To move the title placeholder, simply click on it while it is selected. Position the title placeholder by holding down the mouse button as you move the mouse. Release the mouse button when you are satisfied with the new location.

HELPFUL HINT

Hold down the Option key to prevent unwanted horizontal or vertical movement when moving a text or graphic element. Holding down the Option key constrains movement to the direction of the first move. Thus, if you start to move the title placeholder up, you cannot inadvertently move the title placeholder sideways.

Selecting line and paragraph spacing

Notice the almost exaggerated line spacing between the two lines in the title placeholder. To adjust this, once again, open the Text menu and select "Line spacing."

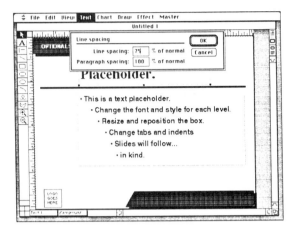

Persuasion's "Line spacing" command permits you to fine tune the distance between lines of type and paragraphs.

The "Line spacing" dialog box allows you to specify spacing between lines which are wrapped between lines as well as add extra space between text separated by a hard return.

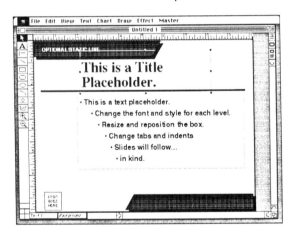

Title placeholder after reducing line-spacing and repositioning.

Notice how much better the title placeholder appears if you reduce line spacing to 75%. Select the title placeholder once again and re-position it slightly lower. It now fits between the horizontal accent line and the trapezoid at the top of the slide.

HELPFUL HINT

As type size increases, you might want to get in the habit of reducing line-spacing. This saves vertical space and—more important—allows you to create titles and paragraphs which appear as more distinct visual units.

The line spacing control offers you far more control over line and paragraph spacing than using the Return key. The Return key—in effect—adds a fixed amount of space, equal to a blank line of text. Line spacing, however, because it is based on percentages of the type size chosen, is far more precise.

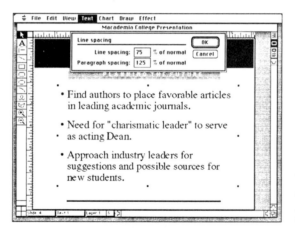

In general, reducing line spacing and increasing paragraph spacing helps separate the ideas.

Extra space between paragraphs can improve the readership of subheads containing text which extends over two, or more, lines. By reducing line spacing within each subhead, and increasing paragraph spacing between each entry, the entries will emerge as distinct visual units.

Alignment options

With "This is a Title Placeholder" still selected, open the Text menu, hold down the mouse button and scroll down until you reach "Alignment." You will now be presented with a list of alignment options.

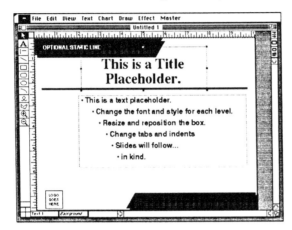

Centering the title within its placeholder.

Select "Centered" and release. The text in the title placeholder will now appear centered between the handles which indicate the size and position of the placeholder.

HELPFUL HINT

Remember that the "Alignment" you choose is relative to the size of the placeholder, as indicated by the eight handles—or dots— indicating its size and placement. Text centered in an off-centered box, for example, will not be centered on your slide or overhead.

Formatting subtitles

After you have chosen typeface, type size, type style and alignment for titles, repeat the same steps for Slide master subtitles.

In many cases, you may choose a smaller size of the typeface chosen for the title, although you might add visual interest by setting the subtitle in italics. By restricting title and subtitle to the same typeface, you can choose a more contrasting typeface for the body copy that follows.

Formatting textblocks

As you formatted titles and subtitles, you became exposed to Persuasion's basic text formatting tools. The only tools not introduced were tabs and indents. These are used to format body text placeholders.

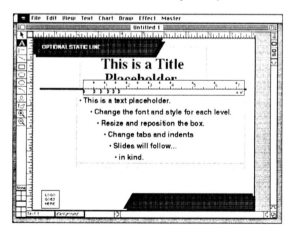

Slide master with body text placeholder and "Show text ruler" selected.

Return to your Slide master and click on "This is a body text placeholder." This is where you can individually format each subhead level of your body copy. Each subhead level can be formatted with its own tabs and indents, typeface, type size, and type style.

Now, select the textblock, beginning "This is a text placeholder" under the horizontal line below the title placeholder. Notice how each level of subhead is indented an equal amount to the right.

To adjust tabs and indents for all, or each level of subheads, select the "This is a text placeholder" text block and choose the "A"—or Text tool—at the left-hand side of the screen. Highlight the line, or lines, you want to fine-tune by holding down the mouse button as you drag the cursor through them.

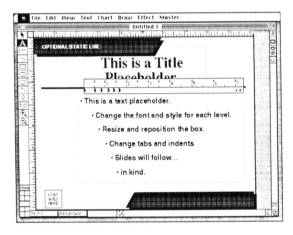

Selecting multiple subhead levels for formatting.

Notice how the highlighted lines appear either in reverse, (white type against a black background). or appear against a different colored background, depending on the type of Macintosh and monitor you're working with.

Hanging indents may be used at any subhead level.

When you select "Show text ruler" from the Text menu:

- The downward-facing arrows at the top, above the ruler, indicate tabs for the various levels of subheads.

- The upward and downward facing triangles below the ruler indicate indents. By moving the lower triangles to the right, you can create hanging-indents where the first line of a word-wrapped paragraph begins to the left of succeeding lines of type.

HELPFUL HINT

After adjusting indents and tabs, click on "Show text ruler" again by opening the Text menu and scrolling down to it. This will de-select it. Otherwise, the rulers will show up every time you click on a textblock or use the Text tool.

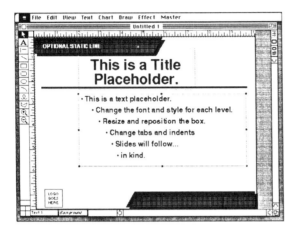

Unformatted body text placeholder.

Next, individually format each subhead level by selecting the Text tool from the left-hand side of your screen, highlighting the level, and selecting one of the formatting options from the Text menu:

- Font—or typeface
- Size
- Style

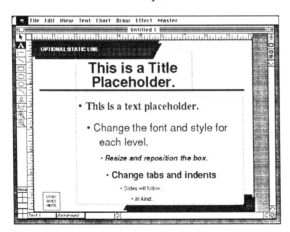

Body text placeholder after individually formatting each level of the outline.

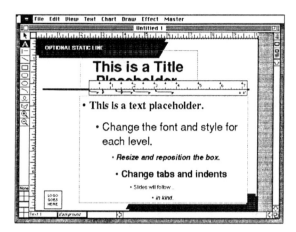

Body text placeholder after adjusting tabs indents.

Persuasion allows you to individually adjust the alignment of each subhead level. Thus, you can justify the first subhead level—that is, set it in lines of equal length—and set the remaining lines flush-left.

Advanced formatting options

The above typeface, type size, type style, line-length and alignment tools are used regardless of whether you're creating a black and white or color presentation. The advanced formatting options described below are of special interest if you are creating color slides or color overheads.

Choosing text color

Once again, select "This is a Title Placeholder." Open the Text menu and scroll down and select "Color."

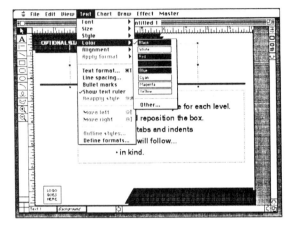

You can choose one of the eight basic colors for text...

You can choose either one of the eight named primary colors.

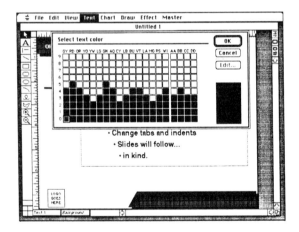

...or choose from a wider selection in the "Set text color" box.

Or, if you have a color monitor, you can choose a particular color by choosing "Other." This offers you a choice of 200 pre-defined colors. Notice how the preview box shows you the particular choice you have made.

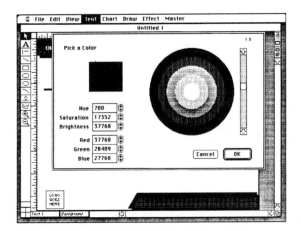

The "Pick a Color" box offers an even wider selection of colors which can be specified by number.

If you choose one of the shades to the right of the wide line, you can click "Edit." This takes you to the "Pick a Color" screen where you can choose any precise shade of color. You can modify the hue, saturation, brightness and precise color balance. You can pick of the three primary colors precisely the hue, saturation, brightness of the colors.

In a similar way, you can select the precise color for text of any, or all, subhead levels.

HELPFUL HINT

As always, restraint is a virtue. Avoid the temptation to include too many text colors in your slides and overheads. Choose colors which form a strong contrast—yet don't "fight"—the Slide master background.

Selecting shadow offset and color

Once again, select "This is a Title Placeholder." After it is selected, choose "Shadow" from the "Style" submenu located under Text.

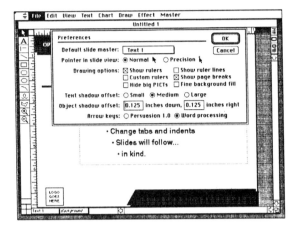

You can adjust the amount of text offset in the "Preferences" dialog box.

Next, open File menu and select "Preferences." Change the "Text shadow offset" from the "Small" default to "Medium."

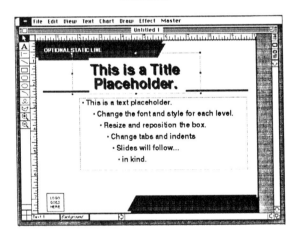

Select "Medium" for a more noticeable shadow effect.

After you click "OK," notice how much more prominent the text shadow appears.

You can add impact to your slide titles by adding a pattern or contrasting color to the shadow, using the "Shadow color" option located in the Effect menu.

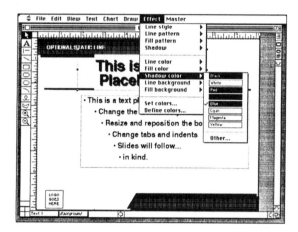

Selecting a shadow color begins with the eight basic colors.

With "This is a Title Placeholder" still selected, choose "Shadow color" under Effects. Once again, you can choose either a named color or a particular color using the "Select color" or "Pick a Color" dialog boxes.

Choosing background colors

Slide titles and subhead text can appear against colored or patterned boxes which contrast with the background slide color you chose in the previous chapter. These color or patterned boxes automatically re-size themselves as you add or subtract words.

HELPFUL HINT

To be effective, text has to form a strong contrast with its background. Shadowed text becomes increasingly useful when text colors approach the colors of their background, i.e. when you're using a light colored text against a light background. When light text is used against a light background, a dark shadow helps the letters pop-out against the background.

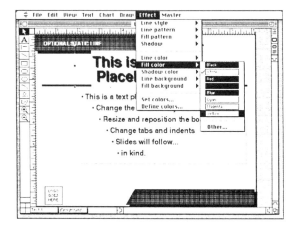

Enhancing text by placing it in a box which contrasts with the Slide master background.

To add a color behind a selected text block, such as the slide title or body text placeholder, select "Fill color" under the Effects menu. As before, you can choose:

- One of the eight named colors
- One of the 200 primary colors from the "Select color" dialog box
- Or you can select a unique color from the "Pick a Color" dialog box

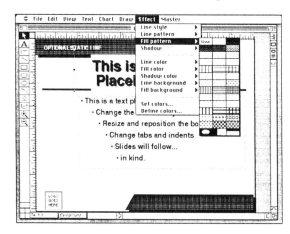

Choosing a pattern for the text box.

Two-color backgrounds

Text backgrounds can contain more than one color. For example, after choosing a desired color from the "Fill color" dialog box, select "Fill background" from the Effects menu. Again, you can choose from:

- One of the eight named colors
- One of the 200 primary colors from the "Select color" dialog box
- Create a unique color from the "Pick a Color" dialog box

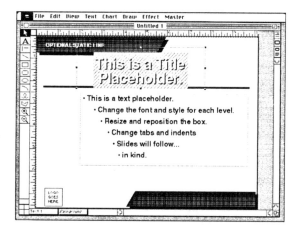

Enhancing text by placing it in a box which contrasts with the Slide master background.

The two colors you have chosen will interact according to the pattern you previously selected. These patterns can consist of horizontal, diagonal or vertical lines, fountain effects or any of the other pattern options accessed through the "Fill pattern" command found under the Effects menu. If you have chosen a left to right fountain effect, for example, the fill color will gradually blend into the background color. If you have chosen a diagonal pattern, the fill color will appear as diagonal lines against the background fill color you have chosen.

Behind all of these, of course, will be the background color of the Slide master created in the previous color. Notice that the size of the text background will expand to accommodate text entered either in the Slide or Outline views.

Text frames and shadows

In addition to allowing you to create one- or two-colored boxes, or "containers" which will isolate a title, subtitle, or body copy from the background, you can also add a frame to the text block. This can be done in either Slide or Slide master view.

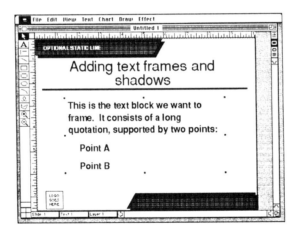

Clicking on a text block selects it for enhancement.

Start by clicking on the text block you want to frame. Then, choose "Line style" from the Effect menu.

- Choose a frame thickness from the left-hand column if you want the frame to be of equal thickness on all four sides.

- If you want to add a vertical feel to your slides, choose a thin line from the horizontal column and a thick line from under the vertical symbol.

- Or, if you want to add horizontal emphasis, choose a thick line from the horizontal column and a thinner line from the vertical column from the "Line style" dialog box in the Effect menu.

Next, choose "Line pattern." If you want a solid frame, click on the black box in the "Line pattern" dialog box. After you have chosen an appropriate pattern, the text block will be framed. This frame will expand or contract to accommodate the amount of text it contains.

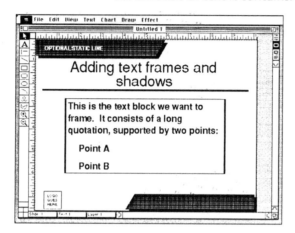

Text block surrounded by a frame with different horizontal and vertical line thicknesses.

While the text block is still selected, you can color the frame by choosing "Line color" from the Effect menu.

You can even go a step further, and surround your text with a patterned, two-color frame. To do this, select "Line pattern" and "Line background" and make your appropriate pattern and color choices.

HELPFUL HINT

Two-colored text frames are often created using the diagonal patterns which point to the upper right of the slide, although the grey shaded options are very popular when preparing black and white overheads.

You can also enhance text boxes by adding a shadow. While the text box is selected, select "Shadow" from the Effect menu and choose a desired shadow pattern. By selecting "Shadow color" from the Effect menu, you can color this shadow.

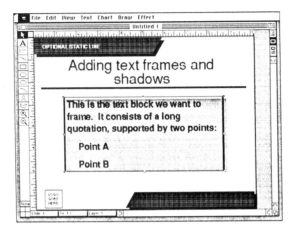

This is what will occur if you add a shadow to a text block without choosing a fill pattern (or choose a fill pattern of "None").

When placing a shadow around a text block, however, you must always provide a fill color, as described above. Otherwise, the background shadow will obscure the letters. This is because Persuasion's shadow is actually a background box the size of the original box.

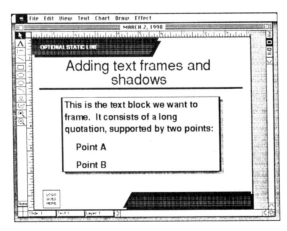

Adding a fill pattern makes a considerable improvement!

Everything is returned to normal when you select a fill color and pattern from the Effect menu--even if the fill color is only white (used when preparing black and white overheads).

Persuasion 2.0, (and following), allows you to control the direction of shadows applied behind objects like text boxes. Select "Preferences" from the File menu. The "Preferences" dialog box allows you to adjust the amount of shadow below and to the right of the object. By entering larger numbers, you can make the shadow more pronounced.

By entering negative numbers, you can make the shadow appear above and to the left of the text box.

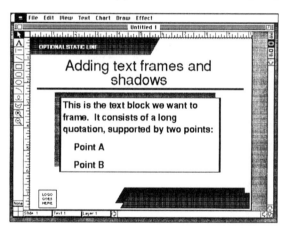

Entering negative numbers in the "Preferences" dialog box relocates the shadow above and to the left.

HELPFUL HINT

Remember that changes made in the "Preferences" dialog box apply to all slides, not just the individual slide you're working on.

HELPFUL HINT

Do not confuse "Object shadow offset" with "Text shadow offset." "Text shadow offset" only controls the amount of shadow behind individual letters. "Object shadow offset" determines the amount of shadow which will be applied behind the text box as a whole, as well as any other objects you might create and add a shadow to.

Formatting bullets

Persuasion also allows you to choose the size and type of bullets used to introduce the various levels of subheads. Click on "This is a text placeholder."

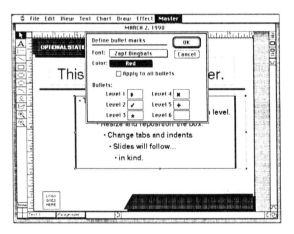

The Slide master "Define bullet marks" dialog box allows you to use different types and colored bullets for each outline level, or none at all.

Select "Define bullet marks..." from the Master menu. You can now choose a different symbol for the bullets introducing each subhead level.

- First, choose the typeface which contains the symbol you want to use for bullets.
- Then, type in the letter, or keyboard combination, which accesses the desired symbol.

If you click on the "Apply to all bullets" option, you only make one choice which will apply to all subhead levels.

HELPFUL HINTS

Use the Macintosh Keycaps desk accessory to locate desired symbols. The Zapf Dingbats collection can be extremely valuable helping you develop a unique "look" for your presentation by using high-character symbols instead of everyday bullets or asterisks.

After choosing the type of bullet desired, you can turn the bullets on or off by using the "Bullet marks" command found under the Text menu.

HELPFUL HINTS

If you want to omit bullets from any particular level, simply select the level in the "Define bullet marks" dialog box and hit the space bar. This eliminates bullets for that level.

Creating and applying formats

As can be seen from the above, text formatting can involve numerous commands accessed through several different menus. To speed up your work, and maintain consistency, Persuasion allows you to create formats which incorporate all of your formatting decisions. These formats can include typeface, type size, alignment, line-length and color decisions.

There are two ways you can create text formats:

- You can format by example, basing a format upon an already-formatted text sample.
- You can format from scratch.

Let's start with "formatting by example."

HELPFUL HINT

The advantage of formatting by example is that it offers the most flexibility: you can incorporate alignment (i.e. flush left, centered, flush right, justified), and line-spacing decisions into your format definitions.

Creating a text format

To reduce a complicated series of text formatting commands to a named and easily-recalled format, choose a slide or Slide master containing text formatted with the typeface, type size, style and color attributes you want to reuse. Select the previously formatted title, subtitle or body text, or placeholder, by clicking on it.

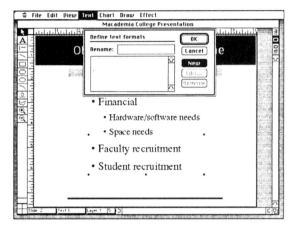

"Define formats" dialog box.

Select "Define formats..." at the bottom of the Text menu.
Click on "New."

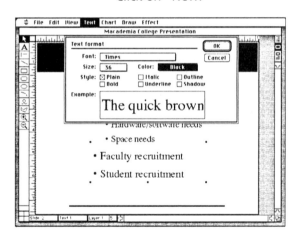

*Your previous formatting
decisions appear in the "Text
format" box.*

The "Text format" box appears, which summarizes your
previous formatting choices. If you still agree with them,
click "OK," (or press Enter/Return).

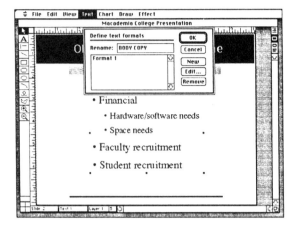

Naming a format.

You are returned to the "Define formats" dialog box. Give the format a name, i.e. "Slide subheads" and click "OK." Typeface, type size, type style and color options have been saved.

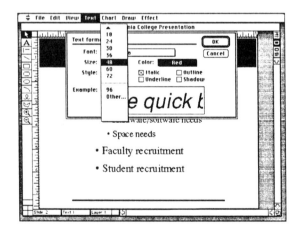

Choosing a type size in the "Text format" dialog box.

To create a format from scratch, start by selecting "Define formats..." from the Text menu. Select "New." Click on "Font" and you will be presented with a list of available typefaces. Click on the typeface you desire. Click on "Size" and "Color" and make appropriate choices. Click on desired style options.

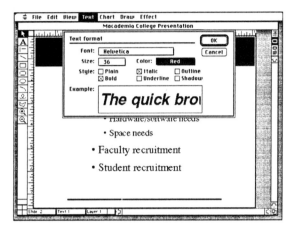

Choosing and previewing text attributes.

Notice that you can preview your choices each time you make a choice in the "Example" window. When you are satisfied with your choice, click on "OK," or Enter/Return.

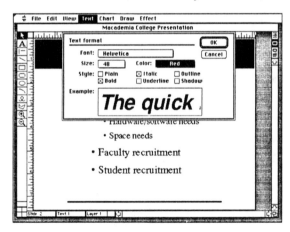

Previewing new text format.

You will then be returned to the "Define text formats" dialog box. Enter a name for the format. Replace the "Format 1" default with a name which appropriately describes the new format. Formats can be identified by:

- Typeface and type size, i.e. "Helvetica 36"

- Typeface, type size and color, i.e. "Helvetica 36 red," "Helvetica 36 blue," etc.

- Function—"Subtitles," "Chart titles," "Level 1 Org Chart," etc.

HELPFUL HINT

Develop a consistent way of naming your text formats, one which can be easily used over and over again. You might consider storing your format names and definitions in a three-ring binder, or on a blank page of the Persuasion documentation, where they will be available for instant reference.

Editing and removing formats

To edit a previously-created text format, choose "Define formats..." from the Text menu. Highlight the format you want to edit and choose "Edit."

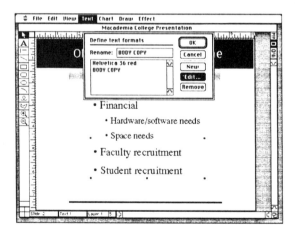

Choose "Edit" if you want to change the attributes associated with a format definition.

Make any desired changes in the "Text format" box and click "OK" (or press Enter/Return).

HELPFUL HINT

Editing a format does not affect previously-formatted slides. You must highlight text and re-apply the re-defined format in either Slide master or Slide views.

To remove a previously-created format, choose "Define formats..." from the Text menu and select the format you want to remove. Click on "Remove." Click "OK," or press Enter/Return. Click "OK" once again in the "Define text formats" box and the format will be removed.

Applying formats to existing text

Existing text can be formatted in either the Slide Master or Slide views. There are two ways you can apply a format to previously-entered text:

- Using the arrow-shaped Selection tool, click on the invisible box which surrounds a title, subtitle, or body copy and choose a format from the "Apply format" dialog box found in the Text menu. This over-rides any previously-existing formatting carried over from the Slide master and changes all of the text in the box.

- You can choose the "A"-shaped Text tool icon from the left-hand of your screen and highlight an individual letter, word or sentence. After the desired text has been highlighted, you can use the previously-defined formats accessible from the "Apply format" command.

Select a title placeholder for formatting by clicking on it.

For example, click on the title in a Slide master. Notice the eight dots which define the area.

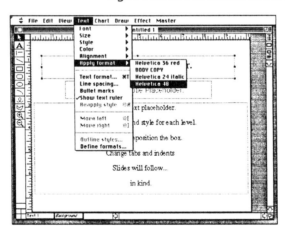

Scroll through your previously-defined formats and choose the desired format.

Select "Apply format" from the Text menu. Hold down the mouse button as you scroll through the list of previously-defined formats and release it when the desired format is highlighted.

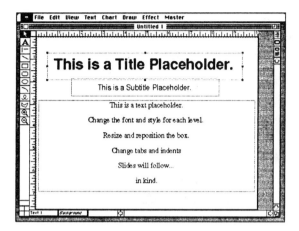

Slide master with newly-formatted title.

The title placeholder will be immediately reformatted when you release the mouse button. Since this was done in the Slide master view, titles throughout your presentation will be reformatted.

HELPFUL HINT

Applying a format to text in the Slide master view formats, or reformats, every slide and overhead based on the master. This makes it easy to quickly make major changes throughout your presentation.

Alternately, you can also use the Text tool in the Slide view to make selective changes to only the individual slide or overhead you're working on.

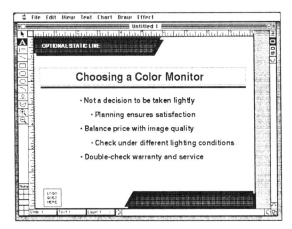

Highlighting text, in this case, the title.

Start by selecting the Text tool icon at the left-hand side of the screen. Double-click on an individual word, or hold the mouse button down as you drag it through a group or words or a sentence. You will know that the text is highlighted when the background color behind the words changes, depending on the type of computer and monitor you're using.

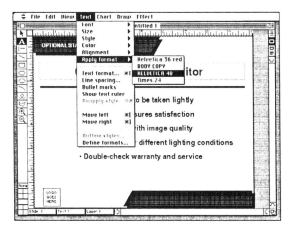

Scrolling through available formats.

Open the "Apply format" dialog box and scroll through the list of pre-defined formats.

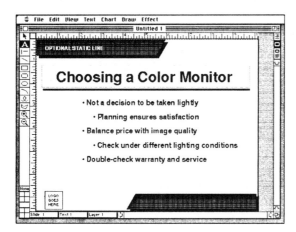

Release the mouse button and the title will be reformatted.

When you release the mouse button, the highlighted text will be instantly formatted.

HELPFUL HINT

Remember that formats applied to an individual slide only affect that slide. Formatting must be done in the Slide master view if you want the changes repeated in every slide.

Applying formats to new text

There are four ways you can format new text in either the Slide or Slide master views:

- You can select a desired format from the "Apply format" dialog box before you enter the text.

- You can highlight the text after it has been entered and then apply a previously-defined format.

- Before selecting the Text tool, you can choose the individual typeface, type size, type size and color attributes you desire.

• You can use the "Text format" shortcut (described below) before you enter the text.

The first, third and fourth options will save you the most time, because you do not have to first enter the text and then go back to highlight it. By selecting a desired format before you enter the text, text will automatically appear in the desired format as you type it.

HELPFUL HINT

Choosing a text format before you enter the text also saves time because there will be less chance that you will inadvertently enter more text than can comfortably fit in the space available for it.

Text format command

The "Text format" command saves time by helping you avoid the necessity of opening the individual typeface, type size, type style and color dialog boxes.

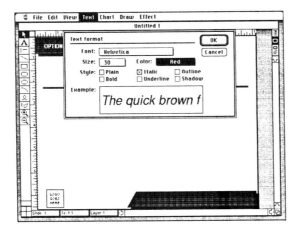

The "Text format" command is a useful formatting shortcut.

The "Text format" dialog box allows you to change all of these attributes at once. You can access the "Text format" command in two ways:

- Selecting "Text format" under the Text menu
- Using the Command T keyboard shortcut

Notice that the "Text format" dialog box provides a preview of the typeface, type size, type style and color you have chosen. This makes it easy to double-check that you have made the right selection.

HELPFUL HINT

Be sure you do not confuse "Apply format," "Define formats..." and "Text format" commands.

- *"Apply format" assigns a previously-defined set of text attributes to either new or existing text.*
- *"Define formats..." permits you to create or edit a permanent set of formatting text attributes.*
- *The "Text format" command is a simple, one-time formatting shortcut which is not saved. Creating a new "Text format" erases the previously-created one.*

Superscript and Subscript feature

The enhanced "Style" offerings found in Persuasion 2.0, (and following), makes it easy to create fractions.

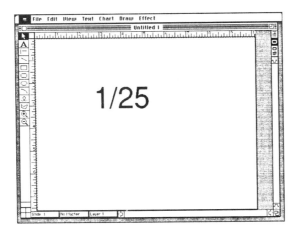

Conventional fraction created with slash.

Start by entering the text as you normally would. Select "Plain" from the Style submenu of the Text menu—or use the Command + Shift H keyboard shortcut. Highlight the "1" and select "Superscript" from the Style options—or use the Command + Shift H (for high) keyboard shortcut. Finally, highlight the "25" and select "Subscript"—or Command + Shift L (for Low).

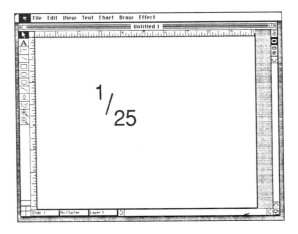

Better-looking fraction created using superscript and subscript numbers.

Superscript and subscript numbers are automatically formatted at approximately 7/12's normal size.

Anchoring text

Persuasion's "Anchor placeholder..." command determines the direction the slide title and body text will "grow" when more than one line of text is added.

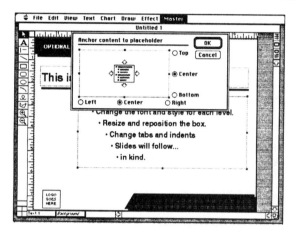

Anchoring text determines what direction the placeholder will move when additional text is entered.

Select the body copy placeholder, (or slide title placeholder) and choose "Anchor placeholder..." from the Master menu. Your options include:

- Text anchored to the center of the text block, which increases equidistantly to the top and bottom of the placeholder as more and more words are added

- Text which grows from the bottom left of the slide towards the upper right

- Text which grows from the bottom right towards the upper left

- Text which grows horizontally from the center of the slide towards the left or right.

- Text which grows vertically from the center of the slide towards the top or bottom of the slide.

The "Preview" box reflects your choices.

You can see the effect of these changes by choosing the Outline view and typing in a sample subhead. As more and more text is entered, the placeholder grows in the direction indicated.

Adding text to individual slides

There will be times when you will want to add text to just one slide. For example, you might want to create a caption for an imported graphic or create a call-out—a phrase next to a chart or graph.

To add text to a single slide, select the Text tool from the icons at the left of the screen and drag it as far to the right as you want the text to appear.

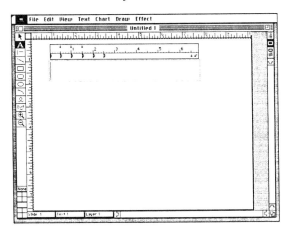

Entering text by dragging the Text tool as far to the right as desired.

Type the new text. Format it by either using a defined format or by highlighting it and choosing the "Text format" shortcut described above.

Editing text

Aldus Persuasion allows you to edit text in either Outline or Slide view. When editing titles, subtitles or text originally entered in Outline view, these changes will flow back and forth. Thus, editing changes made in the Slide view will be reflected in the Outline, and editing changes made in Outline view will be reflected in the Slide view.

HELPFUL HINT

The only editing changes which are not linked between Slide and Outline views are those made to captions or other passages added to individual slides using the Text tool.

There are two ways you can select a word for deletion or replacement:

- Select the A-icon Text tool and double-click on the word
- Select the A-icon Text tool, click before the word and drag the Text tool through the word, holding down the mouse button, highlighting the word.

Highlighted words can be cut, or more suitable replacement words typed right on top of them.

When more than one word is involved, select the Text tool, click on the space before or after the phrase, and highlight the selection by dragging the Text tool through it while holding the mouse button down.

Keyboard shortcuts

Persuasion 2.0, (and following), incorporates several keyboard command shortcuts which can help you quickly locate an insertion point to enter new text or highlight text for deletion, reformatting, replacement, or relocation.

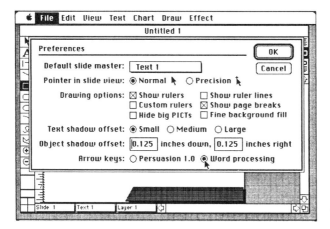

Selecting "Word processing" in the "Preferences" dialog box changes the way the Arrow keys select text.

To access these important new commands, select "Preferences..." from the File menu and locate the "Arrow keys" options on the last line. Click on "Word processing." The Arrow keys can now be used in conjunction with the Shift and Option keys to quickly move the cursor through previously entered text and highlighting desired text.

Here is a summary of the more important Arrow key command shortcuts available when the Text tool and "Word processing" has been selected:

WORD PROCESSING KEYBOARD SHORTCUTS

- **Advance one word to the right:** Hold down the Option key while using the Right arrow key.

- **Advance one word to the left:** Hold down the Option key while using the Left arrow key.

- **Highlight one word at a time to the right:** Hold down the Shift and Option keys while using the Right arrow key.

- **Highlight one word at a time to the left:** Hold down the Shift and Option keys while using the Left arrow key.

- **Advance to end of paragraph:** Hold down the Command key while using the Right arrow key.

- **Advance to beginning of paragraph:** Hold down the Command key while using the Left arrow key.

- **Highlight remainder of paragraph:** Hold down the Shift and Command keys while using the Left arrow key.

The word processing keyboard shortcuts can significantly speed your work.

HELPFUL HINT

Selecting the Word processing option for Arrow keys in the "Preferences" dialog box changes the keyboard commands for toggling between Outline, Slide and Notes views. Instead of using the Command key in conjunction with the Right or Left arrow keys, you now use the Command key plus the Greater than (>)or Less than (<) keys.

Checking for proper spelling

Persuasion's built-in spell checker makes it easy to avoid embarrassing errors. The spell checker will go through your entire presentation and alert you if it encounters any strange or misspelled words.

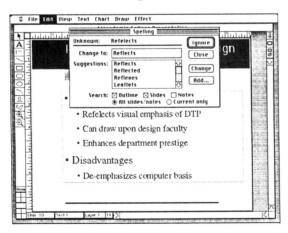

Persuasion's spell checker shows you the exact location of the misspelled word in a slide, note or outline.

There are two ways to activate Persuasion's spell checker facility:

- Select "Spelling" under the Edit menu.
- Use the Command 9 keyboard shortcut.

You can check the spelling of all slides and notes, or just the the portion of your presentation you're presently working on. Whenever it encounters an unknown word, the spell-checker will offer you suggested alternatives.

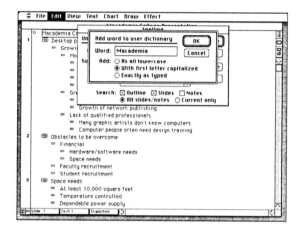

Adding a proper noun to Persuasion's user dictionary.

You can also add words to Persuasion's user dictionary. This prevents the spell checker from stopping in the future at frequently-encountered technical terms or proper nouns associated with your firm or group.

Using the Find/Change command

Persuasion's "Find/Change" command, located in the Edit menu, permits you to quickly locate slides containing specific occurrences of a word—or portions of a word.

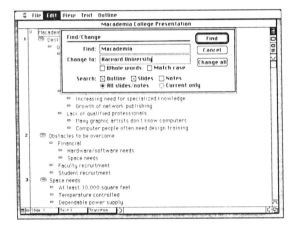

Using Persuasion's "Find/ Change" command to update and reuse a presentation.

You can search for specific occurrences throughout your presentation or just in outline, slides, or notes.

Once located, these words can be automatically replaced by new words. This feature makes it easy to reuse and update presentations by replacing the dates of the presentation or the name of the audience with new information.

Creating text builds

Builds help you introduce information on a logical, sequential basis. Builds focus your audience's attention by preventing them from reading ahead of you. Builds permit the orderly one-at-a-time introduction of items in a list.

There are two ways you can incorporate text builds into your presentation:

- You can add builds to your Slide masters using the "Build layers..." command.

- You can create builds on individual slides by highlighting text and using the Layer pop-up menu at the bottom of the page.

To use builds throughout your presentation, start by choosing the current Slide master. Select the body text placeholder. Click on the "Build layers..." command found under the Master menu. Choose between one and six layers. Click "OK" and return to the Outline view. All slides subsequently based on this master will automatically include builds.

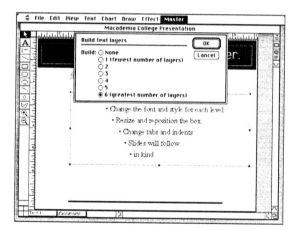

The "Build layers..." command permits you to add text builds to Slide masters.

Enter text. Be sure you do not include more subheads than the number of layers you have chosen.

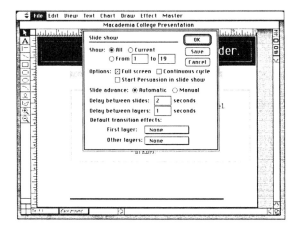

Persuasion's "Slide show" dialog box permits you to review your work and preview builds.

To preview your work, choose "Slide show..." from the File menu. The Slide show can run itself or you can advance through the builds by clicking on the mouse button. Notice that you can preview just the current slide or your entire presentation. As the Slide show demonstrates, each outline level is introduced one at a time.

HELPFUL HINT

You'll probably find that clicking on "Current," rather that specifying a range for slides, will save time reviewing your work.

Builds can also be added to individual slides. Start by highlighting the first text block you want revealed. Open the Layer pop-up menu at the lower right of your screen. Select "Layer 1."

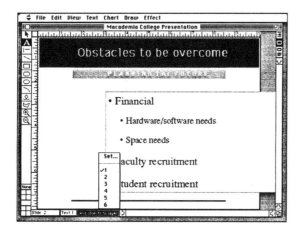

Placing highlighted text on the first layer of a build means it will appear when the slide appears on the screen.

Select the next text block you want revealed. Once again, open the Layer pop-up menu and select the layer where you want to assign the text. Repeat an many times as desired.

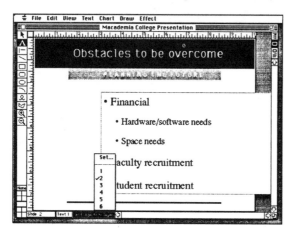

Text placed on subsequent layers will follow.

As you select each text element, notice that a small number to the right of the "Layer" pop-up command indicates the currently assigned layer.

HELPFUL HINT

When creating builds on individual slides, make sure that builds have not already been added to the Slide master. This can cause erratic results.

You can be very creative in your use of builds. For example, instead of introducing information on a line-by-line or subhead-by-subhead basis, you might begin a slide by introducing your major conclusions, followed by the supporting information which you used to develop your ideas.

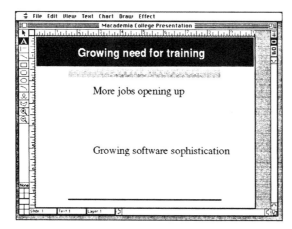

Start by displaying your conclusions...

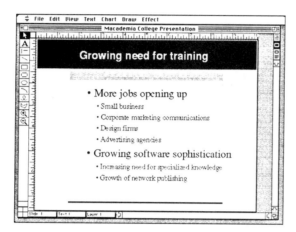

...and follow-up with supporting information.

Builds can be produced as individual slides or overheads. Builds tend to work smoothest when used on 35mm color slides as you can introduce new build levels by advancing the slide carousel forward. Each build level will be properly placed on the screen. Builds are a bit more awkward when used on overhead transparencies, as you have to smoothly remove one transparency while replacing it with another— without causing the image to jump around on the screen.

Builds come into their own when used with computer-based, on-screen presentations. Indeed, as shown in Chapter Nine, Persuasion permits you to include a variety of dramatic transitions between slides and slide layers.

Adding text defaults to AutoTemplates

In the previous chapter, we saw how to store Auto-Templates with colored Slide master backgrounds and graphic enhancements—like borders—added to various categories of Slide masters.

By using Persuasion's "Save as..." command, you can enhance previously-saved AutoTemplates by re-storing them with updated text formatting information. You can store ready-to-apply text formats and Slide masters enhanced with appropriate backgrounds, borders, builds and shadows. This will greatly speed your work. Open the AutoTemplates, and you can immediately get down to business.

To re-store an updated version of a previously-stored AutoTemplate:

- Select "Save as..." and enter the name of the presentation you previously chose.
- Check "AutoTemplate" once again.
- Click on "OK," or press Enter/Return.

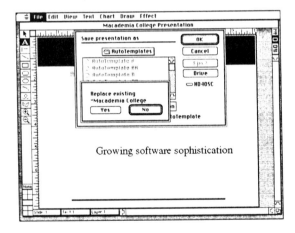

Persuasion verifies that you, indeed, want to replace your previously-created AutoTemplate file with a new version.

You will be asked to verfy that you want to over-write the previous AutoTemplate with your newly formatted text. (This prevents you from accidentally re-formatting an AutoTemplate.)

Click "OK," or press Enter/Return.

The next time you open the AutoTemplate, slide title and body copy text placeholders formatting will remain intact.

You will be able to use the "Apply format" command to format text. The text default will be the same as the last time you used the "Text format" command.

CHECKLIST: EVALUATING YOUR USE OF TYPE SUPPORTED BY PRINTER, FILM RECORDER OR SERVICE BUREAU

1) *Have I chosen typefaces appropriate for my presentation media?*

_____

2) *Have I chosen typefaces appropriate for my message and the atmosphere I'm trying to project?*

_____

3) *Have I chosen a type size appropriate to my audience's reading distance?*

_____

4) *Have I exercised restraint in my choice of typefaces, type sizes and type styles?*

_____

5) *Have I chosen typeface colors that permit words to clearly emerge against contrasting backgrounds?*

_____

6) *Have I avoided over-use of type style attributes, like italics, underlining and shadow text, that can interfere with readability?*

_____

(continued)

Use this worksheet to make sure that your use of type is consistent with your presentation's goals.

7)   Have I modified line and paragraph spacing so that subheads, lists and outline levels emerge as distinct visual units?

_____

8)   Have I created text formats for the various categories of slide architecture to save time and ensure consistency?

_____

9)   Have I used builds to introduce information on a sequential basis?

_____

10) Have I re-stored my presentations as AutoTemplates with formatted text (using the "Save as..." command)?

_____

Typographic choices checklist, continued.

Review and looking forward...

At this point, you have organized the content of your presentation, created a consistent presentation format, and chosen how words will be selectively emphasized. Words can only go so far in communicating information, however.

In the next two chapters, we'll look at two ways you can further enhance the power of your presentation. First, we'll see how easy it is to create high-impact charts and graphs using Persuasion's built in charting tools. Next, we'll investigate Persuasion's ability to import and modify previously-prepared artwork. We'll also see how

Persuasion's drawing tools can be used to enhance charts and graphs as well as imported clip-art.

In the next two chapters, many of the concepts introduced in this and the previous chapter are used over and over again. These include the use of placeholders and the creation of pre-formatted Slide masters for various categories of charts and graphs. In a similar way, you can use slide builds to introduce information into charts, graphs and tables on a step-by-step basis.

Chapter ive:

Using charts, graphs and tables to bring numbers to life

Charts and graphs permit you to present complicated information in an eye-catching way. Even the dullest numbers take on a new life when translated into interesting charts and graphs. Persuasion's built-in charting and graphing facility makes it easy for you to present or compare information in memorable ways. Persuasion also makes it easy for you to create attractive, easy-to-read tables which make it easy to compare information in parallel columns.

The Fifth Step in creating a powerful presentation involves adding graphics. Aldus Persuasion allows you to enhance your words with a variety of graphic formats, including :

- Numbers translated into a variety of charts and graphs
- Information presented in table form
- Relationships visually displayed in organization charts
- Information graphics created with drawing programs and scanned images

In this chapter, we'll survey Persuasion's charting, graphing and table creation tools. In the next two chapters, we'll survey Persuasion's drawing tools and see how they can be used by themselves or in conjunction with previously-prepared graphics files—including clip-art—to enhance charts and graphs created with the tools described in this chapter.

There are four steps involved in supporting your words with powerful visuals:

- Choose the right type of chart, graph or table
- Define chart formats and create Slide masters
- Create individual charts, graphs and tables
- Refine and enhance the charts, graphs and tables

Step One: Choosing the right type of chart or graph

Persuasion can create eleven basic types of visuals. In addition, Persuasion Version 2.0, (and following), allows you to overlay two types of charts or graphs, creating composite visuals which can—for example— visually communicate both comparisons and trends.

All of the chart and graph examples that follow are based on the same Persuasion Data sheet. (Entering information in the Data sheet is described later in this chapter.)

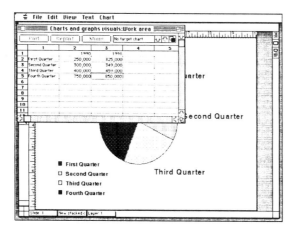

The chart samples on the following pages show the many different ways the information in this Data sheet can be illustrated.

Pie charts

Pie charts permit you to compare part/whole relationships within a single data series.

Use pie charts to display part/whole relationships of a single data series. At a glance, your audience will be able to understand how individual parts relate to the whole. The proportional contributions of each part will be dramatically visible. In the example above, you can show how each quarter's sales contribute to the yearly total.

HELPFUL HINT

Pie charts can only show one series of information at a time. However, two pie charts can be placed side-by-side on the same slide. This is how you could compare 1990 and 1991 quarterly sales using pie charts.

Bar charts

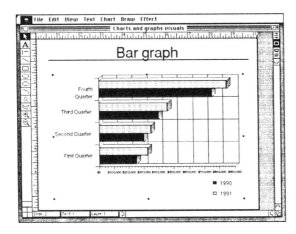

Bar charts permit you to compare more than one data series.

Use bar charts when you want to emphasize comparisons of two or more data series. In the example above, your audience will be able to quickly see how each quarter's sales compare to each other.

Stacked bar charts

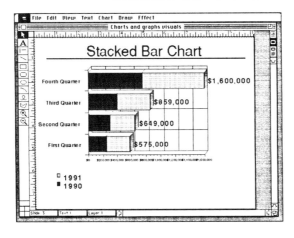

Stacked bar charts display totals.

Stacked bar charts show comparisons as well as totals. In the example above, you can compare each quarter's sales for each year as well as see each year's total sales. Each quarter's two-year sales are automatically totalled at the end of each bar.

Column charts

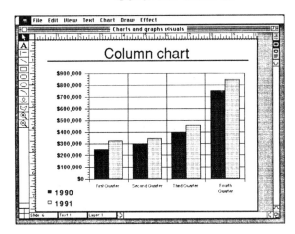

Column charts make side-by-side comparisons easy.

Column charts permit comparisons of categories of information. For example, the above column chart makes it easy to compare each year's quarterly sales figures.

Stacked column charts

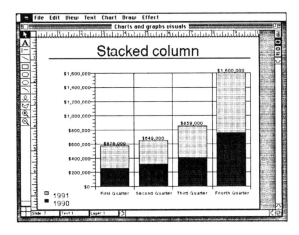

Column charts make it easy to compare categories of information.

Stacked column charts display both part/whole relationships as well as totals. In the example, you can see each quarter's comparisons for each year, as well as compare quarterly sales for the two-year period.

Persuasion automatically computes two-year totals for each quarter.

Line graphs

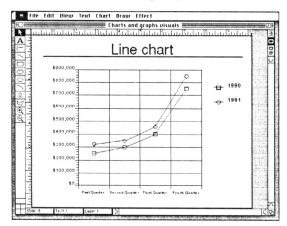

Line graphs display trends.

Line, or fever charts, are ideal for displaying trends over time. One, or more, series of data can be displayed at a time. In the example above, you can see easily grasp the ebb and flow of each quarter's sales totals for each year.

Area charts

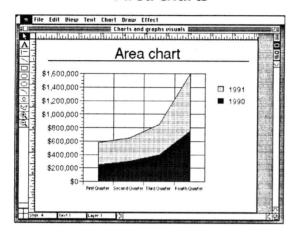

Area charts display both trends and totals.

Area charts display both trends and totals. In the example, you can see the trends of each quarter's sales as well as quarterly totals for the two year period. Persuasion automatically creates the totals.

Scatter charts

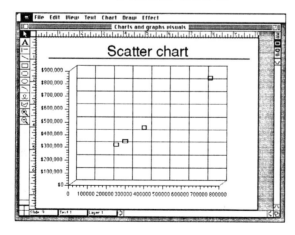

Visual—example

Scatter charts show the distribution of numbers.

High-low

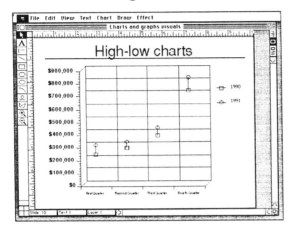

High-low charts permit you to focus on differences in the data range.

In the example, the high-low chart permits you to compare the range of each each quarter's sales.

Tables

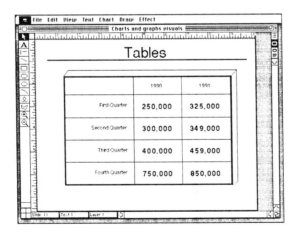

Tables permit you to display a lot of information in a limited space.

Tables display detailed information in parallel columns. Tables are useful when both comparisons and individual words or numbers are important. Whereas charts and graphs sacrifice details for broad, overall impact, tables allow viewers an opportunity to examine individual details.

Organization charts

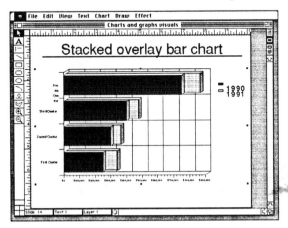

Use organization charts for displaying responsibility and sequence.

Use organization charts to display subordinate/dependent relationships. Organization charts are ideal for displaying levels of authority. They can also be used to display sequences—the steps involved in producing a desired result or how individual contributions result in a finished product.

Stacked overlay bar charts

Stacked overlay bar charts can be used to create three-dimensional charts.

Persuasion 2.0, (and following), allows you to create overlay charts. For example, each quarter's 1990 sales can be placed

in front of 1991 sales. This helps compare yearly performance figures by quarter, although you are not able to see
the two-year totals for each quarter.

Stacked overlay column charts

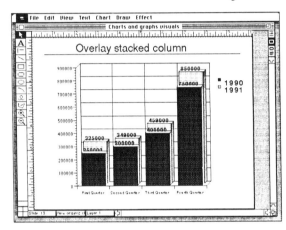

Stacked overlay column charts
can be used for dramatic
displays of rising sales.

Likewise, columns can be placed in front of each other,
instead of totalled.

Overlay area charts

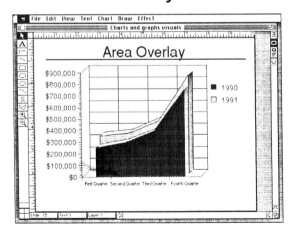

Stacked overlay charts add an
extra degree of tangibility to
data.

Like overlaid column and bar charts, stacked area charts emphasize comparisons but do not provide automatically-computed two-year totals.

Overlaying different chart types

Persuasion also allows you to combine two or more types of charts on a given slide. For example, you might place a line chart in front of a stacked bar chart to emphasize totals.

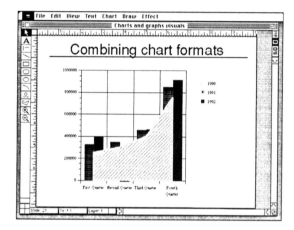

Overlay charts can be used to compare both trends and the performance of individual departments.

Step Two: Defining chart formats and creating Slide masters

There are three ways you can add charts, graphs and tables to your presentation.

- You can add charts, graphs and tables to individual slides, directly entering information into Persuasion's Data sheet or importing information from previously-created spreadsheets.

- You can create pre-defined chart, graph and table types which can be applied to information entered into Persuasion's Data sheet or imported from a spreadsheet.

- You can create Slide masters which contain pre-defined chart types.

Slide masters save you the most time in the long run, because these make it easy to reuse your work at a later date.

What's involved...

Formatting charts, graphs and tables involves:

- Defining text attributes, such as typeface, type size, style, color and alignment

- Choosing desired line styles, fill patterns, colors and shadows

- Determining chart size and placement

Defining charts, graphs and tables involves choosing and naming specific types of charts, graphs or tables, each one incorporating:

- Unique typeface, type size, type style and text color attributes

- Specific line widths and colors

- Previously-determined background colors and patterns

Slide masters contain placeholders for the previously-formatted charts, graphs and tables. Slide masters define the size and location of the visual relative to slide title, subtitle, background and borders, plus any repeating elements—like client or presentation date or information.

Formatting

Formatting visuals is based on single, double or triple-clicking.

Formatting can be done at either the Slide master or individual slide level.

- Clicking once on a chart or graph permits you to delete, resize, or format the entire chart or graph.
- Double-clicking permits you to format a part, section, or category of information presented in a chart, graph or table.
- Triple-clicking selects an individual part of a chart, graph or table.

HELPFUL HINT

Single and double-clicking are typically used when defining chart types and formatting Slide masters. Triple-clicking is most often used when refining the appearance of a specific chart or graph on an individual slide.

Single-clicking

When you single-click on a chart or graph, for example, you can:

- Move or resize the chart either proportionately or stretch it either horizontally or vertically (depending on chart content and slide titles and any other text which will accompany the chart).
- Proportionately resize it by holding down the Shift key as you move one of the corner buttons.

- Add a three-dimensional effect by selecting "Show depth" from the Chart menu.
- Turn on and off chart attributes like "Show depth" (which adds a shadow effect), "Show legend" (which helps identify chart segments) and "Show value labels" (which adds the exact numbers corresponding to the individual columns and bars).

By single-clicking on a chart, graph or table, you can also:

- Choose the typeface, type size, type style and type color for all text included on the chart, graph or table.
- Select line size, line color as well as fill patterns and colors and shadow color for the entire chart or graph.
- Determine chart attributes, such as whether or not totalled values and the legend will be shown.

Double-clicking

Double-clicking allows you to format parts of a chart or graph. For example, double-clicking allows you to:

- Format the text used in either the X- or Y-axis.
- Format the text in a specific level of a table or organization chart.
- Format a chart's legend or value labels.

Triple-clicking

Triple-clicking, described later in this chapter, allows you to format individual elements of a chart, graph or table—for example, individual segments of a pie chart or individual bars in a bar graph.

By triple-clicking on a text element and choosing the A-icon Text tool, you can also edit or reformat legends or X- and Y-axis information.

Defining chart formats

In order to avoid designing charts and graphs from scratch each time you need one, you can pre-define chart formats and assign them to Slide masters. By going through this two-part process, you can create high-impact slides by directly entering the data in Persuasion's Data sheet or or importing data from previously-created spreadsheets.

- The first step is to define a chart format.
- The second step is to place the pre-formatted chart on a Slide master.

The purpose of chart formats is to be able to quickly and easily recall charts and graphs which have been colored and/or shaded with desired attributes. Chart formats also define the appearance of legends, value labels, background grids and X- and Y-axis information.

Just as previously-formatted text can form the basis for a text format, you can base chart formats on previously-drawn charts.

Start by clicking on the prototype chart—either one which has been formatted as desired or a new one created from words and numbers entered into Persuasion's Data sheet—as described in the following section.

While the chart is selected, choose "Define formats..." from the bottom of the Chart menu. Provide the chart with a name—perhaps "B&W PIE CHART." (If you are working in color and have chosen special colors for the chart, you could call it "COLOR PIE."

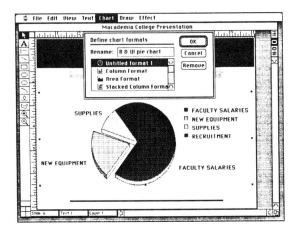

Saving a chart as a defined format allows you to quickly recall it along with desired formatting instructions.

The next time you are plotting a chart in Persuasion's Data sheet and select a chart format, the name of the custom format will appear above the list of ten default formats.

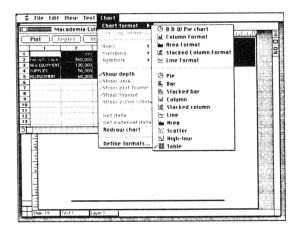

Applying a pre-defined chart format while working with Persuasion's Data sheet.

Creating a Slide master

The next step is to create a Slide master which contains a previously-defined chart format.

Choose "Slide master—Current." Select "Go to master" from the View menu and select "New."

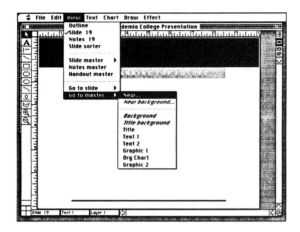

Choosing Go to master—New

Name the new master, perhaps "Pie Chart," and click
"OK."

From the Master menu, choose the elements you want
included on the pie chart master. These may include both
a title and subtitle. Click on chart placeholder.

You will be prompted for the number of segments to be
included in the pie chart placeholder. Click on "OK."

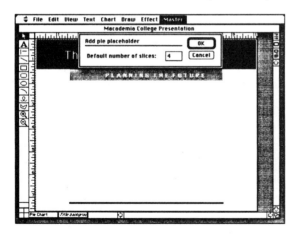

*Choosing the default number
of slices in the "Add Pie Chart"
placeholder.*

When the placeholder re-appears, select the chart. Open
"Chart format" from the Chart menu and select one of
your previously-defined formats. Return to Slide view.

Applying the pie chart Slide master

To put the pie chart placeholder to work, select "New" from the "Slide number" pop-up menu. When the new slide appears, select "Pie Chart" from the "Slide master" pop-up menu.

Data entered in Persuasion's Data sheet will automatically appear in the pie chart format.

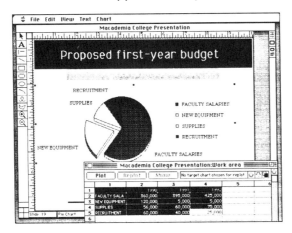

The pie chart Slide master automatically formats data entered in Persuasion's Data sheet. (Note: pie charts only format the first column of data.)

Formatting options

The following are some more examples of the formatting flexibility Persuasion offers you.

Select "Numbers" from the Chart menu and you can format numbers as currency, (i.e. $ 1,000), percentages or in scientific notation. You can indicate whether or not you want negative numbers introduced by hyphens or surrounded by parentheses. If desired, Persuasion can automatically add commas at intervals of one thousand. You can also specify the number of decimal points you want.

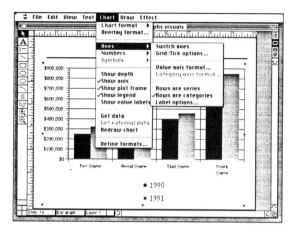

The following charts illustrate how the "Switch axes" command can display the information in this bar graph in different ways.

One of the most powerful formatting commands is the "Axes" command located in the Chart menu. Its submenu contains seven options.

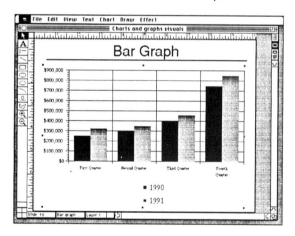

Persuasion's "Axes" dialog box permits you to alter the appearance of your chart.

Click on "Switch axes," and your information is presented from a totally different perspective.

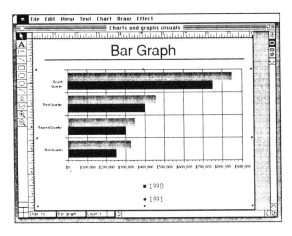

The "Switch axes" command provides a different view of your data.

If you then select "Grid/Tick options...," you can add or subtract background rules which can provide a frame of reference, permitting more accurate comparisons. Tick marks can be added.

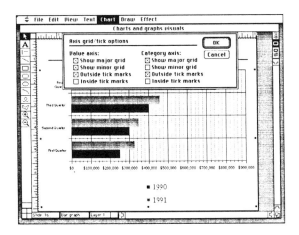

The "Grid/Tick options..." command allows you to add background rules for more accurate comparisons.

When extreme accuracy is required, select "Show value labels" from the Chart menu. Persuasion will indicate the exact numbers represented by each bar or column.

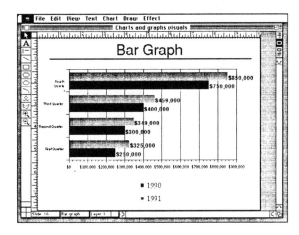

When selected, "Show value labels" includes the exact figures represented by each bar or column.

HELPFUL HINT

Although the above options are available in both Slide and Slide master views, given the many formatting options available, it makes sense to do as much work as possible at the Slide master level. This permits you to save your choices as AutoTemplates, (described later in this chapter). This will save you a lot of time since you will not have to format your charts and graphs every time you need one. You can get right to work entering numbers or importing data.

Step Three: Entering data

Entering information into the Data sheet

Information for charts, graphs and tables is entered in
Persuasion's Data sheet, located in the File menu.

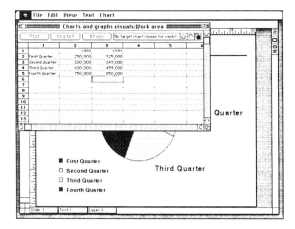

*Data for charts and tables is
typed into Persuasion's Data
sheet.*

The Data sheet resembles an electronic spreadsheet, except
that you cannot compute totals. (Persuasion automatically
computes totals, and adjusts axis information, when
preparing stacked bar or column charts.) Type desired
information into rows and columns.

HELPFUL HINT

*When entering information into Persuasion's
Data sheet, the Return key advances you to the
next row down in the same column. The Tab key
moves you horizontally to the next column in
the same row. If you hold down the Shift key as
you enter Return you advance one row up in the
same column. Holding down the Shift key while
using the Tab key moves you to the left in the
same row.*

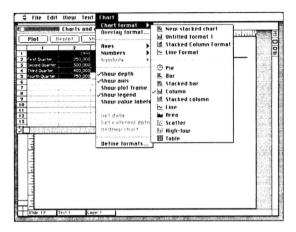

Choosing an appropriate chart format.

Highlight the information and select "Chart or Overlay format" from the Chart menu. Scroll through the list of the ten basic chart alternatives as well as any previously-formatted types of charts. When you have chosen the appropriate type of chart or overlay format, click on "Plot."

HELPFUL HINT

When in Persuasion"s Data sheet, you can view the underlying chart by clicking on the Slide.

The completed chart will appear on the screen, where it can be enhanced as described in Section Four, below.

Importing data from external spreadsheets

If you desire to base a visual on a previously-created spreadsheet, select the "Open external dialog box" from the Data sheet dialog box. Select the appropriate file and folder, using the Open data sheet dialog box. This retrieved information will automatically be placed in Persuasion's

Data sheet, allowing you to choose the desired type of new or previously-formatted chart or overlay format.

Creating and formatting organization charts

The same basic techniques are used to create an organization chart. From the Slide master view select "New." From the Master menu, select "Add title" and "Add organization chart."

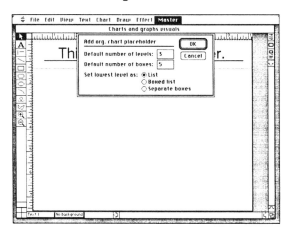

The organization chart placeholder allows you to define the number of levels in the default organization chart and format information in the lowest level.

When the "Add organization chart placeholder" dialog box appears, accept or modify the defaults, and—most important—indicate whether you want the lowest level to appear as a list, a boxed list, or separate box (the default).

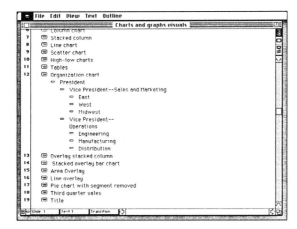

Organization chart information is entered in Persuasion's Outline view.

Organization chart information is directly imported from the information you enter in Persuasion's Outline view.

HELPFUL HINT

Always provide a separate title for your organization charts. This is so the first subhead level of your outline will become the top row of your organization chart. If you fail to provide a separate title, the top row of information will not be connected to the chart that follows.

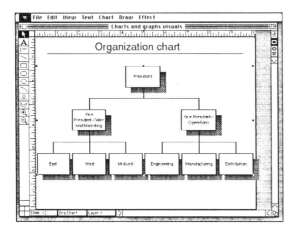

Unformatted organization chart.

Persuasion permits you to extensively reformat your organization chart by single-, double- and triple-clicking. For example:

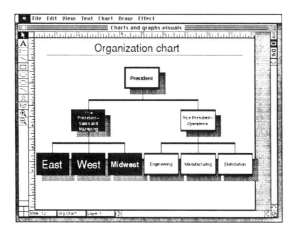

Organization chart after selective formatting.

- By single-clicking on the entire organization chart and choosing "Alignment" from the Text menu, you can center the text in every box. You can also vary the thickness of horizontal and vertical lines, or change background and shadow colors throughout the chart.

- By double-clicking on one of the Organization chart levels, you can manipulate the typeface, type size, type style and alignment of just that level. You can also independently color the lines, background and shadows for each row of your Organization chart.

- By double-clicking on the vertical lines between one layer and another, you can choose a heavier or lighter line from the Effect menu.

- By triple-clicking on an individual entry, you can choose a different typeface, type size, type style, color, background or shadow for just that one box.

Step Four: Enhancing charts, graphs and tables

There are numerous ways to improve the appearance of individual charts, graphs and tables. Most are based on single-, double- and triple-clicking which allows you to choose as much, or as little, of the visual to modify.

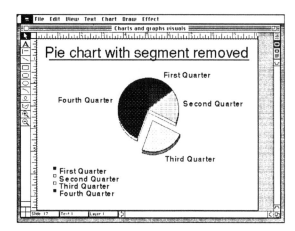

Pie chart with default identification.

For example, you can add visual interest and selective emphasis by double-clicking on one, or more, segments of a pie chart.

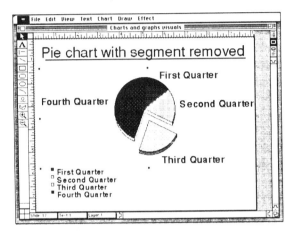

Reformatting text in a pie chart.

You can add even more emphasis by triple clicking on the axis information and selecting a larger type size.

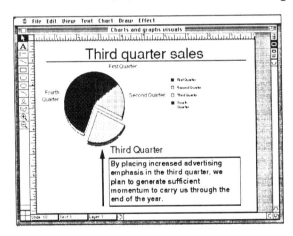

Adding a call-out to a pie chart and increasing the text identifying the emphasized segment.

You can also use Persuasion's Word processing and drawing tool to add call-out's, or detailed explanations to individual segments.

Using builds to enhance charts, graphs and tables

You can enhance the power of your presentation by introducing the various elements of a chart or graph on a step-by-step basis. This prevents the audience from reading ahead of you. You can:

- Selectively introduce segments of a pie chart
- Introduce layers of an organization chart one by one
- Allow the different layers of an overlay bar or column chart to selectively appear on the screen

Builds are based on double and triple-clicking to select different categories of information or segments of a chart or graph and applying each to a different layer using the "Layer" pop-up menu at the bottom of the screen.

Like the text builds introduced in the previous charter, there are two ways you can add builds to charts and graphs:

- You can add builds to chart and graph Slide masters.
- You can add builds to charts and graphs already placed on individual slides.

Select the Slide master for the type of chart or graph you want to enhance with a build. Click on the chart or graph placeholder. Choose "Build layers..." from the Master menu. Notice that builds can be introduced on a series-by-series or category-by-category basis.

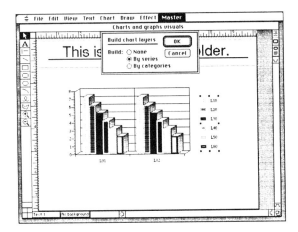

The "Build chart layers" dialog box allows you to specify the order in which information on charts and graphs will be displayed.

For example, if you choose "By series," information will be displayed on a year-by-year basis.

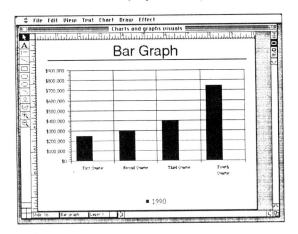

Select "Build—By series," and 1990's sales for each quarter will first appear...

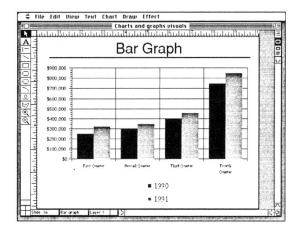

...are followed by 1991's sales for each quarter.

If you choose "By categories," information will be introduced on a quarterly basis.

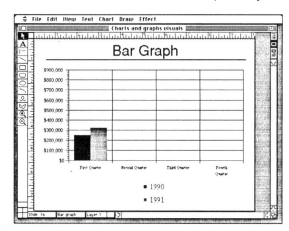

Choose "By categories," however, and First Quarter sales for 1990 and 1991 will be followed by...

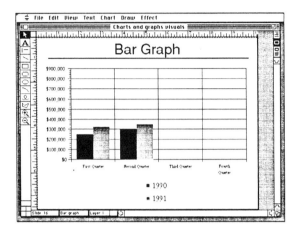

...Second Quarter sales for 1990 and 1991...

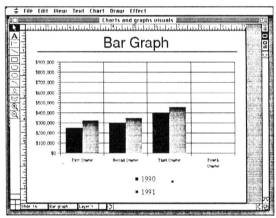

...Third Quarter sales for 1990 and 1991...

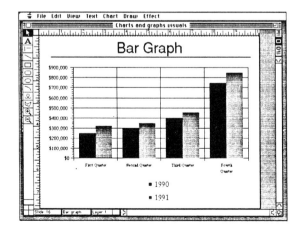

and Fourth Quarter sales for both years.

Although the above six examples offer fundamentally different ways of presenting information, all were created using the same chart type and Data sheet. Persuasion's ability to create eleven types of charts and graphs is obviously enhanced by the ability to add series or category builds to chart Slide masters.

Builds can also be added to previously-created charts and graphs on individual slides in Persuasion's Slide view by triple-clicking on individual segments and assigning them to different layers using Persuasion's "Layer" pop-up menu.

Exporting charts, graphs and tables

You can use Persuasion's Export feature as an adjunct to your word processing or page layout program. Instead of purchasing a separate graphing program, you can export Persuasion charts, graphs and tables as fully-formatted files which can be imported as a graphic into other documents.

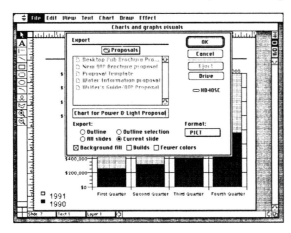

The "Export" dialog box allows you to choose a name and location for saving Persuasion charts and graphs for use with other software programs.

Charts, graphs and organization charts created with Persuasion can be exported to the Macintosh Scrapbook or as PICT files.

> ### HELPFUL HINT
>
> *If you only need to include a completed chart or graph, be sure to disable builds when exporting a Persuasion-created file. Otherwise, each layer of the chart or graph will be saved as a separate image.*

If you are a PageMaker user, you'll find that Persuasion makes a perfect companion program. Just as PageMaker pages saved as Encapsulated PostScript files can be added to Persuasion slides and overheads, Persuasion charts and graphs can greatly enhance PageMaker publications. This synergism multiplies your creative satisfaction and production efficiency.

Adding charts and graphs to AutoTemplates

At the end of the last chapter, we described how you can use Persuasion's "Save as..." command to update a previously-created AutoTemplate file by re-saving the AutoTemplate after you have added defined text formats and created Slide masters for various text categories.

You can repeat this process, after you have created Slide masters for the types of charts and graphs you are likely to use over and over again. You can update a previously-created AutoTemplate by adding chart and graph definitions and Slide masters.

Once again, the procedure is based on Persuasion's "Save as..." command. Enter the name of the previously-created AutoTemplate. Click on "Replace" when you are prompted whether or not you want to replace the previously created AutoTemplate.

SELF-EVALUATION WORKSHEET

1) Did you choose the right type of chart, graph or table to communicate desired information?

_____

2) Have you chosen the right type face, type size, type style, alignment and color for the legend as well as X- and Y-axis information?

_____

3) Did you use builds to progressively introduce information in charts, graphs and tables?

_____

4) Are charts, graphs and tables large enough to be easily understood by everyone in your audience?

_____

5) Did you provide a title for every slide containing a visual?

_____

6) When appropriate, have you included two charts on a single slide to facilitate comparisons?

_____

(continued)

Use this checklist to evaluate your use of charts and graphs.

7) Have you enhanced charts and graphs by double-
   and triple-clicking to format individual segments or
   categories of information?

   _____

8) Have you avoided choosing chart colors which
   fight, or blend into, Slide master background
   colors?

   _____

Checklist continued.

Review and looking forward...

At this point in the preparation of your presentation, you have already entered and formatted words as well as translated numbers into visually-compelling visual images. Most of the information you want to communicate may already be present on your slides and overheads.

In the following chapter, we'll look at ways to add a whole new dimension of impact and communicating power to your presentation using Persuasion's drawing tools. These tools can be used to provide a framework to further enhance your words and visuals, they can be used to enhance artwork created with other programs, or they can be used, by themselves, to create exciting drawings.

Chapter Six:
Creating persuasive drawings

With Persuasion's drawing tools, you can enhance your slides and overheads with accents and borders, add call-out's, create drawings and information graphics, as well as import, resize, modify and re-color previously-created graphics. Persuasion's extensive drawing and coloring tools are enhanced by grids, alignment, and layering capabilities which permit you to work with extreme precision. In addition, Persuasion's Zooming capability allows you to work at various levels of magnification.

Persuasion's drawing tools can be divided into two categories: those used for creating new drawings and those used to modify previously-created graphic images.

Creating new drawings is based on two distinct steps:

- Establishing line thickness, pattern, shadow and color defaults and definitions
- Choosing the right drawing tools

When working with previously-created graphics, you must first:

- Import, place and resize the graphics
- Then, ungroup, modify and—if necessary— recolor the graphic

In either case, the last step is to use Persuasion's various Align, Center, Send and Zoom tools to precisely place the drawings on your slide or overhead.

Establishing defaults

The starting point for making the most of Persuasion's powerful drawing tools is to establish defaults which will be automatically applied when you choose one of the line or object drawing tool. Before you select the line, box, circle or polygon drawing tools, choose the desired formatting options from the Effects menu. Persuasion allows you to pre-select:

- Line thickness
- Line color
- Line pattern
- Fill pattern
- Fill color
- Background fill color
- Shadow color
- Shadow pattern
- Background shadow color

HELPFUL HINT

Establishing defaults before you create lines or filled objects saves time because the lines and objects will automatically be properly formatted as you draw them. Otherwise, after creating the objects, you have to select them and individually employ the various commands located in the Draw and Effect menu. This can take far more time.

Choosing line attributes

There are three major line attributes. These attributes define not only the thickness, pattern, color and shadow of individual lines, but how lines will appear when used in objects like rectangles or circles. Lines can be defined in terms of:

- Horizontal thickness
- Vertical thickness
- Pattern
- Shadows

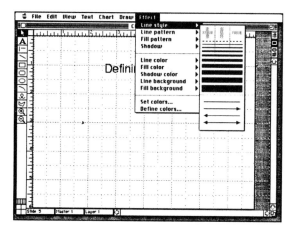

Persuasion's "Line style" submenu allows you to specify different line thicknesses for horizontal and vertical lines.

Line thickness can be identical for horizontal and vertical lines, or you can choose different thicknesses for vertical or horizontal lines. Select "Line style" from the Effect menu. Choose line thickness from the first column if you want the same thickness lines for both horizontal and vertical lines. If you want more flexibility, select different thicknesses for vertical (second column) and horizontal (third column) choices.

HELPFUL HINT

After a line thickness default has been chosen, the pointer of the drawing tool on your screen will automatically display the default horizontal and vertical line thickness you have selected.

Adding arrows

The "Line style" submenu also allows you to specify arrows for lines. Arrows can be pointing left and up, right and down, or in both directions at once.

HELPFUL HINT

Choices made in the "Line style" submenu also influence the thickness of curved lines. You can create arcs which range from thick to thin in thickness by selecting different vertical and horizontal line thicknesses from the Effects menu.

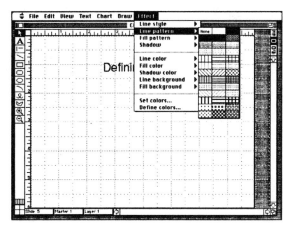

Choosing a pattern in the "Line pattern" dialog box.

Next, select "Line pattern" from the Effect menu. This allows you to specify whether or not you want to create lines out of a solid color, or a pattern created from repeating dots or rules in either one or two colors.

Working with colors

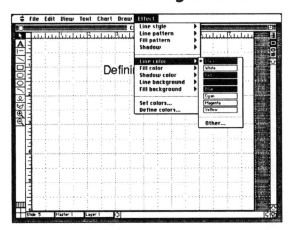

Using one of the eight basic colors to color a line.

Next, select a primary color for your lines. Your first color option is based upon the eight basic Macintosh colors. If you are working with a color monitor and desire a more unique color, click on "Other."

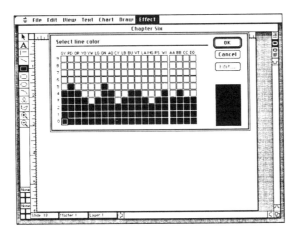

Coloring a line with one of the colors displayed in the "Select line color" dialog box.

The "Select line color" submenu presents you with 200 additional color choices. Select any desired color by clicking on it. Your choice will be shown in the large preview box at lower right.

If you desire an even more unique color, select **any** one of the shades along the right side of the menu and click on "Edit..."

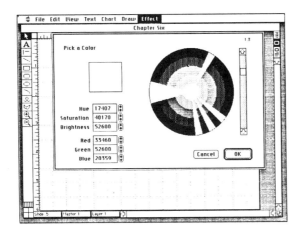

Using the "Pick a Color" dialog box.

This brings you to the Apple Color Picker, where you can select any one of the 16.8 million colors which the Macintosh II can work with. The "Pick a Color" box allows you full access to any desired hue, saturation and brightness. You can select precisely the color and brightness you desire.

- Colors become more saturated—or vivid—as you leave the center of the wheel and approach the circumference. Colors approach gray as you approach the center of the wheel.

- The elevator box along the right of the screen determines how light or dark the colors will be. If you have selected green, for example, light green is at the top of the elevator box, dark green (approaching black) is at the bottom.

As you make your choices, the color you have selected appears at the top of the preview box on the left-hand side of the "Pick a Color" submenu below the original color you have selected for editing. This permits a "before and after" comparison. In addition, the precise Hue, Saturation and Brightness numeric specifications appear in their respective boxes, as does the precise mixture of the three basic colors—red, green, and blue—which specify your choice.

HELPFUL HINT

When selecting one of the Macintosh II's 16.8 million colors, take the time to jot down the numbers which specify your choice. This will make it easy to recreate those colors at a later date.

When you are satisfied with your choices, click "OK." This returns you to the "Select line color" submenu. Again, select "OK."

Choosing a default Line background color

If you selected a patterned line, such as horizontal, vertical or diagonal lines, you can choose a contrasting second color for your lines. Click on "Line background" from the Effect menu. Your initial line color will appear against the background color chosen from the "Line background" submenu. Again, you can choose from the eight basic Macintosh colors or progress to the "Select color" or the "Pick a Color" dialog boxes.

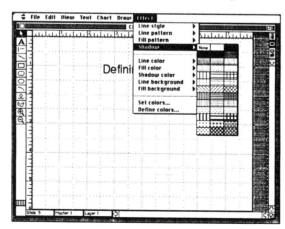

Choosing a line pattern.

Choosing a default shadow pattern and color

Next, select "Shadow" from the Effect menu. This allows you to specify whether you want a white, black, or patterned shadow to accompany lines. If you choose one of the patterned shadows, shadows can be a combination of two colors, as described below.

Just as Persuasion offered you three levels of sophistication in choosing line colors, you can choose colors from either of three shadow color menus:

- The basic "Shadow color" submenu
- The "Select color" submenu
- The "Pick a Color" dialog box

HELPFUL HINT

It's worth taking the time to choose precisely the right shadow color, because the default shadow color you choose also becomes the background for Word processing boxes described in the previous chapter.

Adjusting shadow offset

Select "Preferences..." from the File menu to increase or decrease shadow offset. Separate horizontal and vertical dimensions can be entered in the "Preferences" dialog box. Normally, shadows appear down and to the right. By entering negative numbers, however, you can place shadows above and to the left of lines and objects.

HELPFUL HINT

To remove a previously-applied shadow, select the object and open the Shadow pattern menu. Select "None" to remove the shadow.

Choosing default fill patterns and colors

The final step in establishing defaults for Persuasion's drawing tools is to choose the patterns and colors for the inside areas of enclosed objects, such as circles and squares. As described below, fill patterns can also be applied to partially-enclosed items, like incomplete arcs and incomplete polygons.

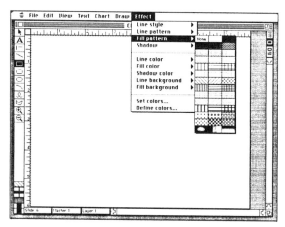

Using the "Fill pattern" dialog box.

Start by selecting "Fill pattern" from the Effect menu. Notice that, in addition to the pattern options offered in the "Line" and "Shadow" submenus, you can create shaded backgrounds with gradual transitions between two colors. These three additional options are located at the bottom of the "Fill pattern" submenu.

Next choose the foreground, or primary fill color. As before, there are three options. You can choose the fill color from the:

- "Fill color" submenu.

- Or, if you select "Other," you can choose a color from the "Select fill color" submenu.

- Or, if you choose a color which can be edited from the right side of the grid, you can select a color from one of the 16.8 million colors accessible in the "Pick a Color" wheel.

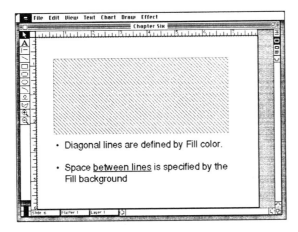

The fill color is the dominant color and appears against the fill background color.

Fills can be created by the interaction of different colors. If you have selected a pattern assembled from lines, the fill color will specify the color of the lines. If you have chosen a dot pattern, the dots will be specified by the fill color you have specified.

These appear against the color chosen in the "Fill background" dialog box.

Specifying and defining colors

In addition to allowing you to establish line thickness, fill pattern and shadow defaults, Persuasion's Effect menu offers a "Set colors" option which permits you to simultaneously choose colors for the six primary colors which define a presentation:

- Text
- Fill
- Line
- Shadow
- Fill background
- Line background

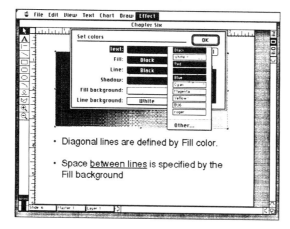

Using the "Set colors" dialog box permits quick access to pre-defined colors.

To use this command, select "Set color" from the Effect menu and, one by one, assign the default colors you desire for each category. In each case, click on the color and either accept one of the eight named Macintosh color or, if you are working on a Macintosh II, select "Other" to advance to the "Select color" dialog box. Or, go one step further and advance to the "Pick a Color" dialog box.

Notice that your color choices are reflected in the preview box located at the right side of the screen.

Another Persuasion shortcut located in the Effect menu allows you to name colors which will later appear in the initial "Line," "Fill," "Shadow" and "Fill color" menus along with the eight basic Macintosh colors. This is a great timesaver, as you will be able to easily locate and instantly choose a precise color shade by a unique name.

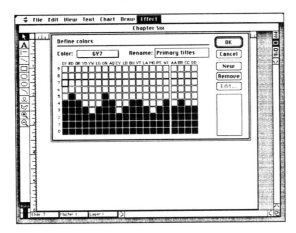

The "Define colors" dialog box offers a wider choice of colors.

Select "Define colors..." found at the bottom of the Effect menu. Select "New." Click on the color which you want to add to Persuasion's basic color menu. Click on the "Rename" box and apply a custom name, i.e. "Primary titles." Click "OK," or Enter, when you are finished.

Repeat the process and create as many named colors as desired. Note that by choosing "Edit" you can advance to the "Pick a Color" dialog box and choose a color for naming from one of the Macintosh II's 16.8 million colors.

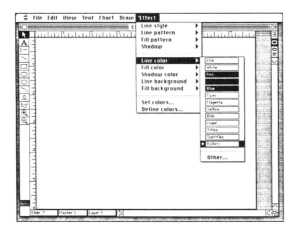

*"Line color" box augmented
with additional color choices.*

The next time you open any of the color menu's, (i.e. "Line," "Fill," "Shadow," etc.), your newly named colors will be present on the list, allowing you to easily select even the most unusual and precisely-specified color.

Previewing defaults

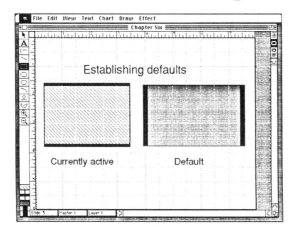

*Note how Persuasion displays
currently active and default
line thicknesses and colors at
the lower left of the screen.*

As you select line and fill patterns and colors, your choices are automatically displayed in the lower left hand corner of your screen. These serve as reminders of your previously-made choices.

HELPFUL HINT

If you change line, fill, or shadow specifications while a tool is selected, however, another box appears at the lower left, on top of the default area. This top box indicates the color and pattern of the currently-selected tool.

In the example above, the default line effects specify thick horizontal and thin vertical patterned rules, yet the currently selected choice calls for a thin horizontal and thin vertical rules. The default fill pattern is a shaded gray, yet the currently active fill pattern calls for diagonal lines.

Choosing the right line drawing tools

Persuasion offers you four line drawing tools. Icons for selecting them are located on the left-hand side of your screen:

- Perpendicular line drawing tool
- Diagonal line drawing tool
- Arc drawing tool
- Freehand drawing tool

The perpendicular line drawing tool is best used for creating independent horizontal or vertical rules, like rules to add impact to titles.

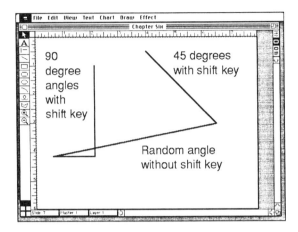

Holding down the Shift key while drawing a line constrains the line to either 45 or 90 degrees.

The diagonal line drawing tool can be used for drawing connected lines at random or specified angles. By holding down the Shift key, you can use the diagonal line drawing tool to draw connected lines at either a 45 or 90 degree angle. Click once each time you want to change direction. Click twice when you have finished drawing the connected lines. (Note: these lines will not be permanently connected unless you group them together, as described below.)

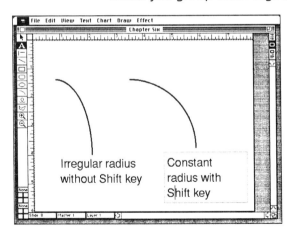

Holding down the Shift key creates an arc of constant radius.

The arc drawing tool can be used to create arcs, or portions of the circumference of a circle. These can be of either constant or varying radius.

HELPFUL HINT

If you hold the Shift key down while using the arc drawing tool, you can create an arc with a constant radius.

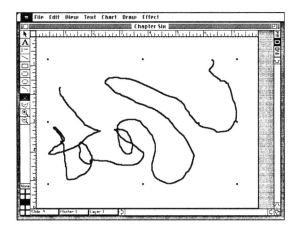

Use the freehand tool to create irregular lines.

The freehand drawing tool can be used, like a pencil, to "scribble" completely unstructured connected lines. There is no need to click every time you desire to change direction: the line will faithfully follow your mouse movements.

Completing arc and freehand drawings

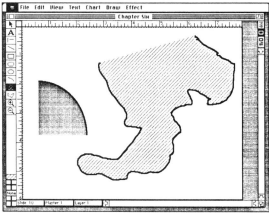

Previously-selected fill patterns automatically create filled arcs and objects when the line drawing tool is used.

If default fill patterns have been previously selected, or are chosen while the arc or freehand drawing tool is selected, drawings will be automatically filled. No additional step is needed.

HELPFUL HINT

If you don't want to fill in your arcs or freehand drawings, and a fill default was previously chosen, while the drawing is still selected choose a fill pattern of "None." This can be done before or after you begin the drawing.

Creating call-out's

You can enhance a chart, graph or other visual by adding call-out's created with Persuasion's line drawing tool. Start by selecting the diagonal line drawing tool. Draw a line pointing to the portion of the graphic you want to emphasize.

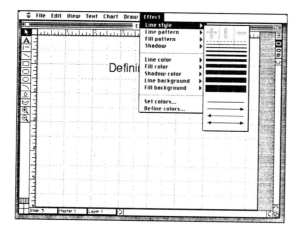

Line color choices also determine how boxes and circles are outlined.

With the line you have drawn still selected—as indicated by the handles at each end—open the Effect menu and select "Line style." Scroll through the various line thickness options displayed in the dialog box and release the mouse button when you come to the line thickness you want.

To add arrows to one end, or both ends, of the line, re-open the "Line style" submenu and click on the option with the arrows pointing in the desired direction.

With the line still selected, click on the Effect menu and select desired "Line pattern." The Pattern dialog box can be used to determine how two-color lines can be created. In this case, click on the diagonal pattern.

Return to the Effect menu and select "Line color." As in the previous chapters, you can choose:

- A named color
- A color from the "Select line color" palette
- A custom-mixed color from the color wheel.

Your choice will be the highlight, or diagonals, in the line you have just drawn.

Next, again return to the Effect menu and select "Line background" and, as above, choose desired color. The color you choose here will appear behind the diagonal pattern.

Creating filled objects

Persuasion offers you four types of object drawing tools which can be used to create six types of objects:

- Used by itself, the box drawing tool creates rectangles.

- You can create squares if you hold down the shift key when using the box drawing tool.

- The rounded corner box drawing tool allows you to create rectangles and squares with different radius corners.

- The polygon drawing tool allows you to create irregularly-shaped objects.

- The oval drawing tool creates either ovals or circles.

Persuasion makes it easy to draw enclosed objects. Start by choosing the box drawing tool from the toolbox along the left-hand side of the screen. Click the mouse on one corner of the square or box you want to draw and drag the pointer to the opposite corner and release it. After completion and while selected—as indicated by the six handles—you can easily:

- Move the object to a new location, by clicking anywhere within the box .

- Change line thickness, color and pattern using the tools found under the Effect menu.

- Select desired shadow thickness, color and pattern, also using the Effect tools.

- Fill the box with the color, or colors, and pattern you desire, again using the Effect tools.

You can also resize the box.

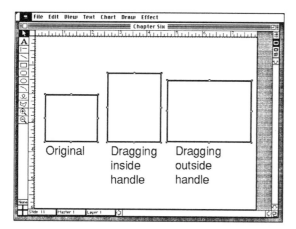

Dragging an inside handle changes one dimension of an object, i.e. height or width. Dragging a corner handle can resize an object in two dimensions.

You can make the box taller, shorter, wider, or narrower by dragging on the inside handles. You can simultaneously adjust the length and width of the box by dragging on one of its corner handles.

Maintaining object aspect ratio

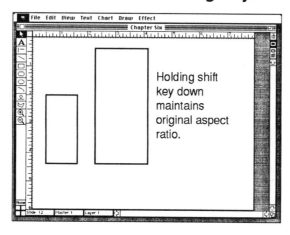

Holding down the Shift key while dragging maintains an object's original height-to-width ratio.

If you want to maintain the boxes original length to width ratio, simply hold down the Shift key as you drag one of the corner handles. This will ensure that the original proportions of the box remain unchanged.

Drawing squares

To draw a square instead of a rectangle, hold down the shift key as you drag the cursor from one corner of the square to the other. This ensures that the four sides of the box will be equally long.

Drawing rounded corner boxes

Choose the rounded corner tool if you want your squares and rectangles to have rounded corners.

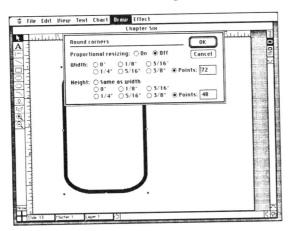

Persuasion allows you to proportionately or disproportionately adjust the corners created with the rounded corner box tool.

Select the "Rounded corner" option under the Draw menu if you want to modify the radius of rounded corner boxes. This option allows you a great deal of customizing ability. You can enter different figures for horizontal and vertical radii. This permits you to create custom effects, ranging from "television picture tubes" to subtle gradations.

Drawing circles and ovals

Circles and ovals are created in a similar way, using the circle drawing tool. Simply click on the starting point you want, move in a diagonal direction and then release the mouse button.

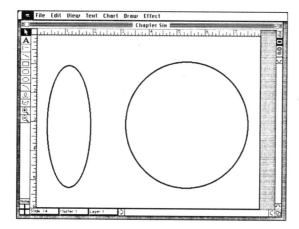

Hold down the Shift key if you want to draw a circle instead of an oval.

If you drag in a primarily drag in a vertical direction, you'll create a vertical oval. If you drag primarily in a horizontal direction, you'll create a horizontal oval. To create a circle, hold down the Shift key while dragging.

Drawing polygons

Persuasion's polygon drawing tool makes it extremely easy to draw multi-sided figures. These figures automatically complete themselves.

Start by selecting the polygon drawing tool and click on the starting point of the figure. Drag the cursor to one of the corners, and click again. Click on each point where the line changes direction. Double-click when you have completed drawing all four, five, or however many, sides of your polygon and have returned to the starting point.

Automatic polygon completion

When drawing polygons, you don't have to connect the starting and ending points. Persuasion will complete your polygon for you.

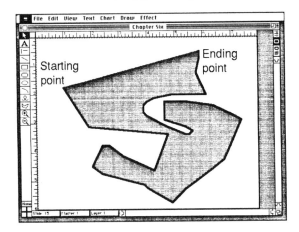

If a fill pattern and color have been chosen, Persuasion automatically finishes polygons for you.

Simply double-click on the last junction point. Persuasion will automatically connect that point and the starting point with an invisible line enclosing either your previously-chosen fill, or a specially-chosen fill. This feature can be used to create some very interesting, almost three-dimensional effects.

HELPFUL HINT

Whenever you have finished drawing a line, box, circle or polygon, immediately deselect the drawing tool by clicking on the arrow, or pointer, too. Otherwise, the next time you click on the mouse you'll begin to create another object.

If this happens, simply double-click and use the Delete key to immediately eliminate the box or polygon you have inadvertently begun to draw. Or, use the Control Z, or "Undo add," command found under the Edit menu.

Modifying and recoloring lines and objects

After creation, you can again use the tools found under the Effect menu to choose line thicknesses, colors, fills, patterns and shadow effects. Select the lines or objects you want to modify or recolor and use the various commands located in the Effect menu.

Grouping and regrouping

Persuasion's "Grouping" command permits you to assemble several individual objects into a single object. There are numerous applications for this command. For example:

- By grouping several objects together into a single object, the individual parts cannot become inadvertently separated.

- Grouping permits several objects to be moved together as a single unit.

- You can accurately and simultaneously increase or decrease the size of several objects when they have been grouped together.

- Grouping permits you to create logos and other specialized artwork.

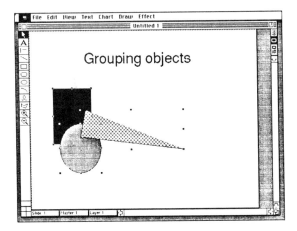

Three objects, each surrounded by their own handles.

To group two, or more, objects together, hold down the Shift key while clicking on them. Or, using the Shift and Selection tool, select them by surrounding them with a flashing marquis box. Then, select "Group" from the Draw menu—or use the Command G keyboard command.

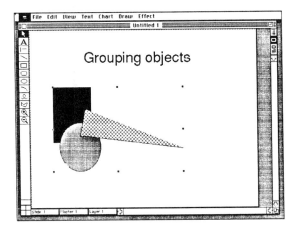

Single object surrounded by just one set of handles.

Notice that handles indicating the original objects have been replaced by eight handles surrounding a single grouped object.

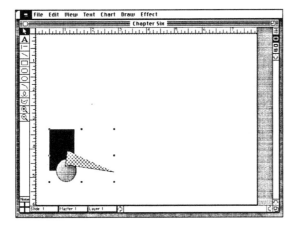

Grouped objects moved and resized as a single object.

You can now move the original objects as a single unit as well as distort or resize the object as a single unit.

Ungrouping and regrouping

If you are not happy with your composite creation, select the object and select "Ungroup" from the Draw menu—or choose the Command U keyboard shortcut. Individual handles now, once again, surround the original objects.

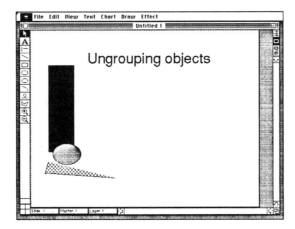

Enlarging the rectangle after ungrouping.

You can now selectively move or resize individual segments which previously comprised the grouped object.

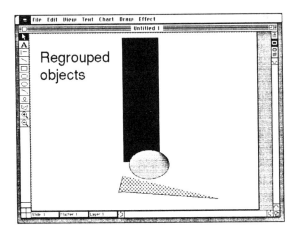

Relocating the regrouped object.

After moving or resizing selecting and moving one or more individual objects, select the "Regroup" command from the Draw menu, or use the Command R shortcut. After regrouping, the objects can, again, be moved, resized or distorted as a single object.

HELPFUL HINT

Ungrouping and regrouping are often used to make permanent changes in a chart, graph, table or organization chart. Ungrouping permits you to remove and resize a segment of a pie chart. Regrouping permits you to subsequently resize the modified pie chart while maintaining the original proportions and relationship of the chart to the enhanced segment.

Working with imported art

To import a previously-stored graphic image, select "Import" from the File menu and select the drive and folder containing the file. You will find hundreds of quality images in the "Art of Persuasion" files which accompany Persuasion 2.0.

Importance of file compatibility

Just as your typeface choices are limited by the ability of your output device to reproduce them, you must make sure that the output device being used to reproduce slides and overhead transparencies can print your graphics files.

- If you are using a PostScript printer like an Apple LaserWriter II NT, for example, you can safely use artwork created with programs like Adobe Illustrator or Aldus FreeHand and saved as Encapsulated PostScript Files. If, however, you are using a Hewlett-Packard PaintJet printer or are sending your files to Genigraphics or another service bureau, you are unlikely to be pleased with the way Encapsulated PostScript files are reproduced.

- Likewise, the use of paint-type files is limited to PostScript printers.

PICT and PICT2 files are the best choice for optimum reproduction with the vast majority of slide and overhead output devices. These offer the most flexibility for modification and can be reproduced equally well on PostScript printers, a wide variety of color as well as service bureaus. PICT files are created by applications like MacDraw, PICT2 are color files created with applications like MacDraw II. Most of the sample clip-art files included with Persuasion are PICT2 files.

Moving and resizing graphic images

To move an imported graphic, simply click on it and move it to a desired position.

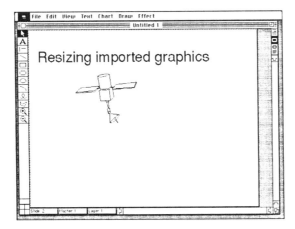

Original object...

To resize an imported graphic, first select the image by clicking on it.

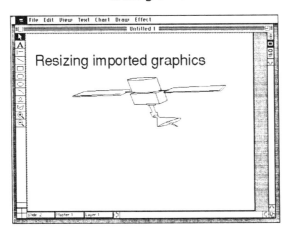

...stretching it horizontally.

To make the image taller, shorter, wider, or narrower, select one of the four inside handles and drag it in the desired direction. This will distort the imaging, changing the aspect ratio, or height to width ratio of the original image.

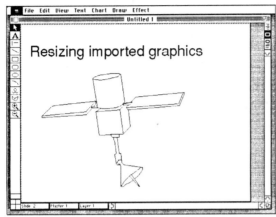

Holding down the Shift key while dragging proportionately increases or decreases an object.

To resize an image without changing its proportions, hold down the Shift key and select one of the four outside corner handles. You can now increase or decrease the image proportionately in all directions.

Modifying and re-coloring imported graphic images

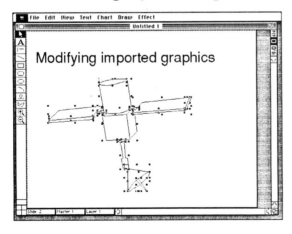

Ungrouping allows you to move, resize or recolor an object's component parts.

Persuasion's "Ungroup" command permits you to greatly modify the appearance of an imported graphic. Start by selecting the graphic. Then select the "Ungroup" command found under the Draw menu, (or use the Command U keyboard shortcut.)

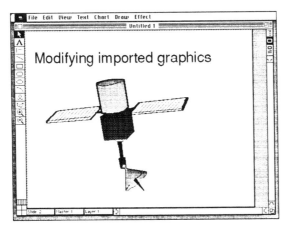

Ungrouping and choosing different fill patterns permits you to dramatically alter the appearance of an imported graphic.

You can now use the following commands found in the Effects menu to completely change the appearance of the graphic. You can:

- Change the line thickness, pattern and color of any component part of the original drawing.
- Change the fill patterns and colors of any segment of the original drawing.
- Selectively shadow any segment of the original drawing.

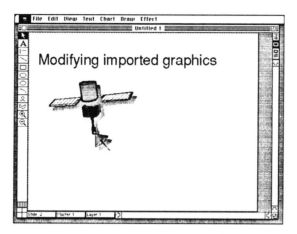

Regrouping permits you to move and resize the imported graphic as a single object.

After the object has been selectively modified and recolored, you can, create a single object out of it by using the "Regroup" command found in the Draw menu—or using the Command R keyboard shortcut. The modified drawing can once again be moved, resized or shadowed as a single unit.

Working with Persuasion's placement tools

Centering objects on a slide

Objects can also be accurately centered on a slide. Objects can be centered horizontally, vertically, or both.

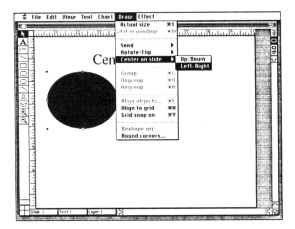

Selecting an object for centering.

Start by selecting the object you want to center. Then, select "Center on slide" from the Draw menu. Choose the option you desire, in this case, "Left/Right," from the submenu and release the mouse button.

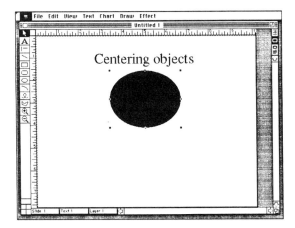

Horizontally-centered object.

Reselect the object and, again, select "Center on slide" from the Draw menu. This time, select "Up/Down."

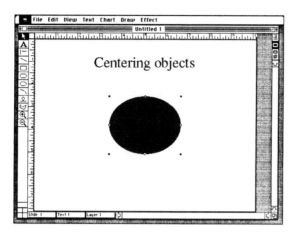

Object centered both horizontally and vertically.

Release the mouse button, and the object will be precisely centered in the slide.

HELPFUL HINT

You can use the "Center on slide" command for text boxes as well as graphic boxes.

Aligning objects

Persuasion's "Align objects..." command allows you to quickly and accurately align two, or more, objects with each other. Both text and graphics can be aligned with this command.

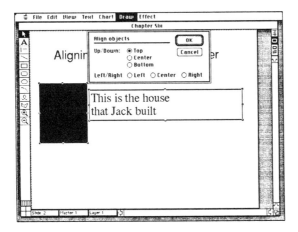

"Before" view; selecting the text and graphic object to be aligned.

Start by holding down the Shift key as you click on each of the elements you want to align. Then, select "Align objects..." from the Draw menu, or use the Command L keyboard command shortcut. Choose the alignment options desired from the "Align objects" submenu and click on "OK," or Enter/Return.

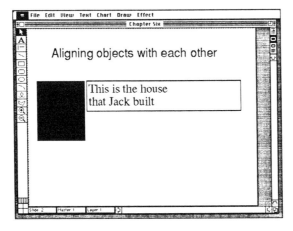

Text and graphic after being aligned at top.

Instantly, the objects will be aligned at the top.

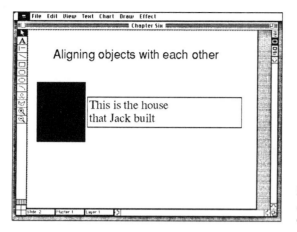

The centers of the text and graphic objects can also be aligned.

Objects can also be vertically centered with each other. Bottom alignment is also possible.

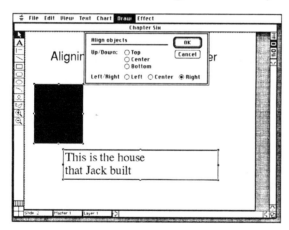

Selecting objects for horizontal alignment.

Two, or more, text and graphics objects can also be aligned horizontally. Start by clicking on each object while holding down the Shift key and choose the alignment option desired.

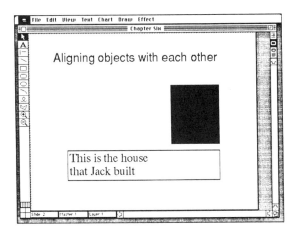

Text and object after right alignment.

Right, left and centered options are also available.

Persuasion's Send command

Persuasion's "Send" command, found in the Draw menu, permits you to layer text and graphics on your slide. This permits you to control the overlap of various objects, so that certain objects appear on top of, or behind, other objects.

Using the "Send" command found in the Draw menu, you can move a selected object:

- To the front or back one layer at a time
- Directly to the topmost or lowest layer

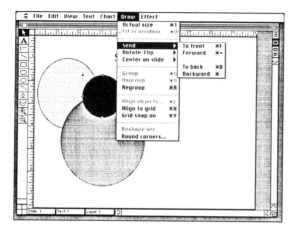

Original object placement, reflecting the order in which the objects were created. Note that the black circle has been selected.

Start by selecting an object by clicking on it. For example, click on the black circle. Open the "Send" submenu and select "Backward," and release the mouse button.

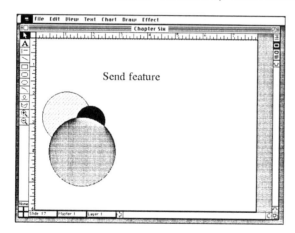

If you select "Send— Backward," the circle will be repositioned one layer back.

The selected object now appears one layer back.

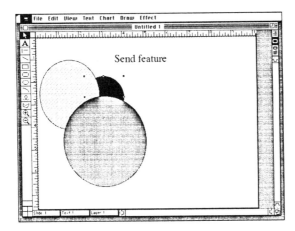

If you select "Send—To back," however, the circle will be repositioned on the lowest level.

If you had, however, selected "To back," the selected object would have been immediately placed on the bottom of the layer.

In a similar fashion, you can advance background objects to the front, one layer at a time, or go directly to the top layer.

HELPFUL HINT

You can save a significant amount of time by making use of Persuasion's Send keyboard command shortcuts: Command F and Command B for, respectively, "To front" and "To back," plus Command = and Command - for, respectively, forward one layer and backward one layer.

Rotating and flipping images

Imported artwork, or objects created with Persuasion's drawing tools, can be rotated and flipped.

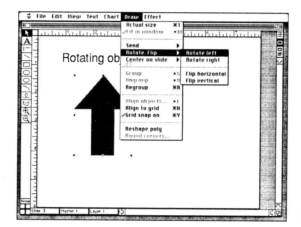

Compare the original graphic...

First select the artwork and—if it is an imported graphic—ungroup it. Select "Rotate/Flip" and choose the alignment option desired.

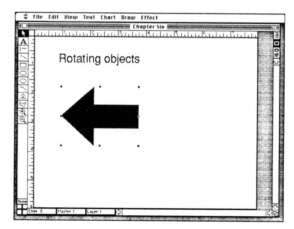

...with the image after it has been rotated to the left.

Objects can be rotated in 90 degree increments.

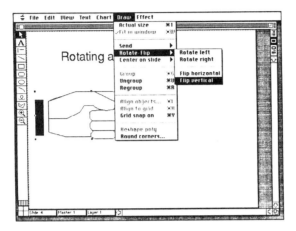

Compare the thumb's location on the original graphic...

You can also turn an object over by selecting it and choosing to flip it horizontally or vertically.

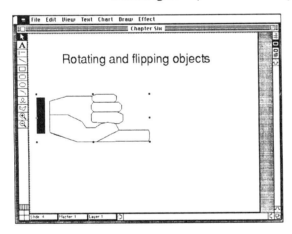

...with the thumb's placement after the object has been flipped.

When used in conjunction with Persuasion's ability to ungroup, modify and recolor imported artwork, Persuasion's "Rotate/Flip" commands permit you to add drama and impact to a wide variety of existing artwork.

> ### *HELPFUL HINT*
>
> *Try selecting "Ungroup" if the "Rotate/Flip" command in the Draw menu cannot be accessed after you have selected an imported graphic object.*

Grid snap on/off

Behind your Persuasion screen is an invisible grid of horizontal and vertical rules. These grids rules can exert a magnetic attraction, helping you easily line-up objects to a common horizontal or vertical location. The "Grid snap on/off" command, located in the Draw menu, allows you to turn this magnetic attraction on or off. Turning it off allows you more precise control of object location.

If you select "Grid snap off," objects can be "near," but not lined-up or touching each other.

> ### *HELPFUL HINT*
>
> *Use Command Y keyboard shortcut to toggle between "Grid snap on" and "Grid snap off."*

Changing screen magnification

Persuasion Version 2.0, (and following), permits you to work at varying levels of screen magnification. When you desire an overall view of your work, you can show your entire slide or overhead on the screen. However, when you want to carefully align objects, you can magnify and focus on just a portion of the slide. Persuasion's Zoom feature thus permits you to work with extreme accuracy.

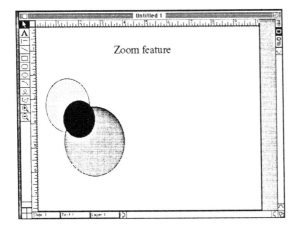

Compare the size of the original screen image...

To zoom in on a portion of your screen, click on the magnifying glass icon containing the plus sign on the left hand of your screen.

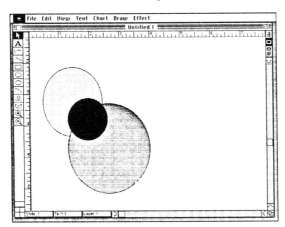

...with the image after clicking once on the Zoom icon.

Position the magnifying glass over the portion of the screen you want to view in great detail and click.

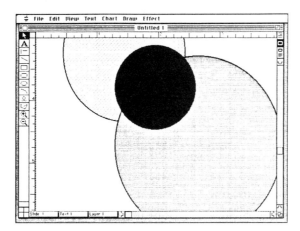

*Click once again on the screen
while the Zoom up icon is
active...*

Click again to move in for an even closer look at your
work.

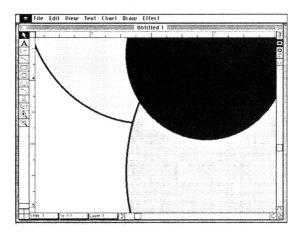

...clicking again...

Click as many times as necessary to achieve the desired
level of magnification.

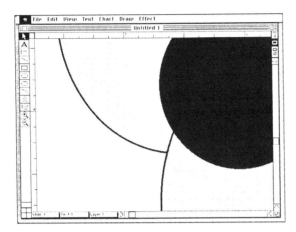

...and click once again!

At maximum magnification, you can work with great accuracy, adjusting the tiniest details of your presentation.

To return to your original screen view, select the magnifying glass icon containing the minus sign on the left hand of your screen. Position it on the screen, and click. Each time you click, you will see more of your original slide.

HELPFUL HINT

While using either Zoom tool, you can toggle between magnification and reduction by holding down the option key as you click on the screen. This helps you quickly change views without needing to change from the magnification icon to the reduction icon—or vice versa.

DRAWING TOOL CHECKLIST

1) *Have you used Persuasion's drawing tools to create distinctive accents, borders and call-out's?*

   _____

2) *Have you avoided overusing Persuasion's drawing tools to the point that text is hard to read?*

   _____

3) *Have you avoided inadvertently distorting the shape of imported graphics?*

   _____

4) *Did you use Persuasion's "Ungroup" command to modify and recolor imported art?*

   _____

5) *Have you avoided the temptation to overuse clip-art?*

   _____

6) *Are graphics properly centered on the screen?*

   _____

7) *Are graphics properly aligned with adjacent text, charts and graphs?*

   _____

8) *Have you avoided line or object colors which fight or blend into the background?*

   _____

Use this Drawing Tool Checklist to evaluate your use of Persuasion's drawing tools.

Review and looking forward...

By now, your slides and overhead transparencies should be complete. Text, information graphics as well as a variety of accents and original artwork should already be in place.

The next step is to review your work and make sure that your slides and overheads are arranged in the proper order. Persuasion's Slide show feature makes it easy to preview your presentation from the audience's point of view. If any slides or overheads are out of sequence, they can be easily rearranged in Persuasion's Outline or Slide sorter view.

Chapter Seven:
Advanced techniques

In the previous three chapters, we've looked at Persuasion's text, charting and drawing tools in isolation. These tools, however, are rarely used by themselves. In this chapter, we survey some of the ways these tools can be used with each other, and in conjunction with the "Art of Persuasion" clip-art. The following examples are just a preview of the effects you can achieve on your own as you become more familiar with Persuasion.

Your ability to create high-impact slides and overheads is directly proportional to the extent that you combine Persuasion's text, charting and drawing tools. By combining the tools introduced in previous chapters, you can not only greatly enhance the appearance of charts and graphs, but you can enter the world of information graphics: visuals which combine charting and drawing techniques to both communicate and entertain at a glance.

Let the following serve as an introduction to a continuing self-education process which you'll follow on your own, letting your creative instincts guide your way.

Enhancing charts and graphs

Even the best charts and graphs can be improved. Here are some ways you can enhance their impact.

Increasing text legibility

As a starting point, let's see how various Persuasion text and drawing tools can be used to improve the appearance of a chart and graph.

In the example below, because of the many digits in the value labels—the totals at the top of the columns—your audience would probably find it difficult to read the individual totals in the bar chart below.

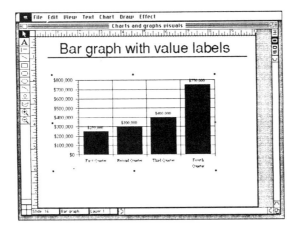

Original bar chart showing totals.

If you tried increasing the size of the numbers by double-clicking on them and choosing a large "Size" from the Type menu, the numbers would be partially obscured by the bars. (Furthermore, if two data series were included, the numbers would undoubtedly run into the adjacent bars.)

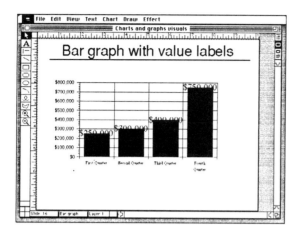

Simply increasing the size of the type isn't enough, as the bars obscure the totals.

The solution involves four steps:

First, ungroup the chart so you can separately format each element of the chart.

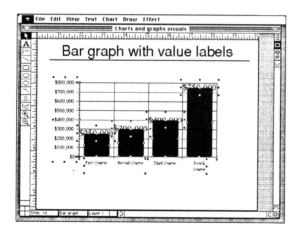

After ungrouping the chart, the totals can be raised above the columns.

Second, raise and align the numbers for each category by clicking and raising them by dragging. (If multiple data series were being displayed, the "Align objects..." command could be used so that the totals for each data series would appear on a common horizon.)

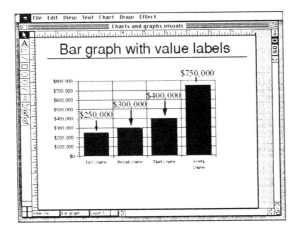

Adding pointed arrows.

If necessary, use the Text tool to increase their size even larger.

Next, choose a suitable line thickness and arrowhead from the Effect menu and connect the resized numbers to the columns of the chart.

Finally, "Regroup" the chart so that value labels will be updated if you replot the chart after changing some of the numbers in the Data sheet.

As you may have noticed in the above illustrations, the information along the bottom axis appears very small. If you double-click on the bottom axis information and increase its size, "Fourth Quarter" becomes broken vertically.

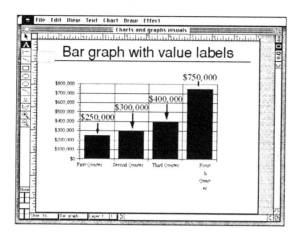

Increasing X-axis type size often causes undesirable word breaks.

You could try triple-clicking on "Fourth Quarter" and entering a hard Return, but Persuasion's chart text formatting commands don't permit this.

A better solution is to:

- Select Persuasion's Text tool.
- Highlight "Fourth Quarter."
- Delete the text.
- Re-set "Fourth Quarter" using Persuasion's Text tool—(the A-icon located along the left-hand side of the screen.) Persuasion's Text tool allows you to enter the required hard Return necessary to place "Fourth" and "Quarter" on separate lines.
- You'll probably notice that "Quarter" is too far down from "Fourth." To eliminate this unsightly gap, choose "Line spacing" and choose "Paragraph spacing" of 75%. This will tighten up the gap.
- Finally, if necessary, hold down the Shift key while double-clicking on both horizontal axis information and the new "Fourth Quarter." Use Persuasion's Align to Top tool to make sure the new "Fourth Quarter" is is aligned with the original three.

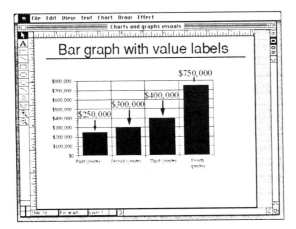

Resetting X-axis information using Persuasion's Text tool permits you to control line breaks.

As you become more familiar with Persuasion, you'll find yourself fine-tuning your charts and graphs using similar techniques.

Adding graduated fills

You can easily transform a "ho-hum" bar or column chart into a visually striking one by replacing solid colored bars with graduated fills.

Although the numbers in the stacked bar chart below are readable, the chart lacks drama and impact. It hardly commands attention. In color, there is a chance the solid fill patterns of the large bars might be overly prominent.

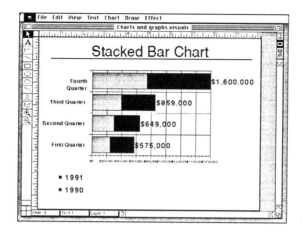

The original chart with solid fills is not as visually interesting as...

One solution involves:

- First double-click on one the 1990 bars—which selects them all—and choose a graduated left-to-right fill pattern from the bottom row of the "Fill pattern" dialog box in the Effect menu .

- Then, select different fill and fill background colors from the Effects menu.

- Repeat by double-clicking on one of the 1991 bars and again choosing a left-to-right graduated fill pattern and two different fill and fill background colors.

The result will be a stacked bar chart with far more visual interest—especially in color!

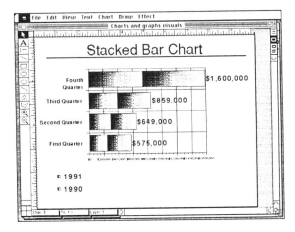

...the same chart with graduated fills.

Creating information graphics with the Art of Persuasion

Persuasion 2.0, (and following), includes a wealth of well-drawn illustrations which can be used to create information graphics—the types which brighten up many of today's daily newspapers and weekly news magazines.

Audience expectation levels are rising as the use of information graphics becomes more and more common. Your audiences are apt to expect the same levels of visual communication in your presentation.

Here's how to create a several information graphics using the "Art of Persuasion" in conjunction with Persuasion's "Copy" and "Paste" commands as well as many chart and drawing tools. The following isn't the only way the graphic could be created, but does illustrate the necessary interplay between numerous tools described in the previous two chapters.

Start by creating a column graph. Not too exciting, is it!

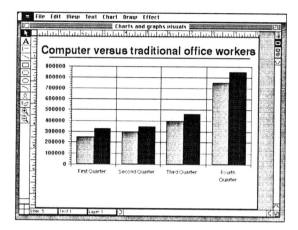

A typical column chart—compare it to the final version on page 291!

Changing column backgrounds

Start by choosing lighter backgrounds for the columns.

HELPFUL HINT

Lighter backgrounds will allow the imported clip-art to stand out better—an especially important consideration if you are preparing black and white media.

Working with clip-art

Then, import an appropriate clip-art illustration from the "Art of Persuasion." Choose "Computer operator" from the "People" folder.

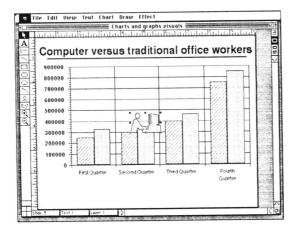

Importing, resizing and recoloring an "Art of Persuasion" illustration included with your software.

- When it appears in the center of the screen, hold down the Shift key and resize it to approximate size—a little less than the width of the columns.

- While it is selected, ungroup it using the "Ungroup" command in the Draw menu.

- While still selected, select a solid fill pattern. (In addition, if you are working in color, choose an appropriate fill color.)

- Regroup the image (so it doesn't come apart while it is being dragged.)

- Drag the illustration into approximate position in the first column.

Again holding down the Shift key, proportionately resize the image until there is sufficient breathing room on either side of it. Then:

- Select "Copy" from the Edit menu.
- Select "Paste."

An additional image will appear in the center of the screen.

Select "Paste" about ten times. These images won't be visible, as they will appear on top of each other in the middle of the screen.

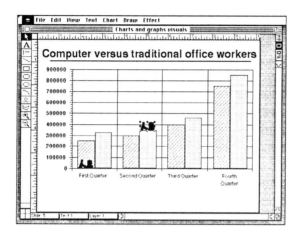

Determine final size by placing the illustration in the column, then create as many additional copies as needed using Persuasion's "Copy" and "Paste" commands.

HELPFUL HINT

Use the Command V shortcut when making several copies of an item. This is much faster than repeatedly opening the Edit menu and selecting "Paste."

One by one, drag and place as many images as necessary into the first column. Try to maintain equal vertical spacing. Place an image at the top of the column, even if it extends beyond the top of the column.

- Click on the images in the first column while holding down the Shift key. Select "Align objects..." from the Draw menu. Align the images Left/Right, Center.

- Drag additional images into the remaining columns of the first series. Click on the images in each column while holding down the Shift key and align the images Left/Right, Center.

Then, click on the images on the bottom row of each column while holding down the Shift key. Select "Align objects..." from the Draw menu. Align the images Up/Down, Bottom. Repeat for each row of images. This ensures that the images in each column will be horizontally aligned.

When you're finished, place an image below the bottom of the chart, for use in the legend. Delete any excess images pasted into the center of the screen.

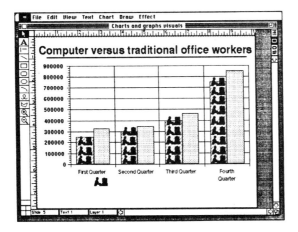

Placing and aligning multiple images in each column and then...

HELPFUL HINT

The vertical placement of the image in the first column defines the placement of the images in the remaining columns. Thus, pay special attention to the vertical spacing of the images in the first column before Bottom aligning them to the images in the remaining columns.

Next, import a second image and repeat the process. Choose "Man at Desk" from the "People" folder.

Ungroup the image after it has been imported. Choose a different fill pattern and color to visually separate it from the first series. Resize the image and make as necessary copies as necessary. Drag the images into position and align them. Again, allow the top images to extend over the top of each column, if necessary. (Don't omit an image, even if only part of it will fit in the column.)

Again, place the last image below the bottom of the chart and delete any extra pasted images remaining in the center of the chart.

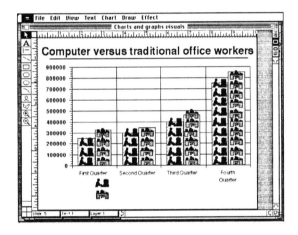

...repeat the process with a different illustration for the second category of information.

Finishing touches

Next, use Persuasion's square corner box drawing tool to create a box at the top of each column. This box will trim the tops of the illustrations which extend above the columns, trimming the images flush with the column tops. Start by setting the box drawing defaults.

- Choose a solid line fill and a line color of white. (If you are working in color, choose a line background which matches the Slide master background fill color.

- Select a solid fill pattern.
- If you are working in color, choose the same fill color used for the Slide master background.

Be sure to make the box large enough to completely cover all of the images extending above the column.

HELPFUL HINT

Use Persuasion's Zoom feature to magnify the portion of the screen you're working on. This will increase accuracy and speed your work. You will probably also find accuracy will increase if you deselect "Grid snap on" from the Draw menu.

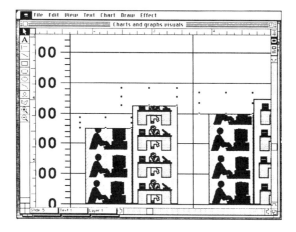

Using boxes with a fill and lines colored the same as the slide background to trim the tops of each column.

In some cases, as shown below, the newly-drawn boxes may cover portions of the background grid.

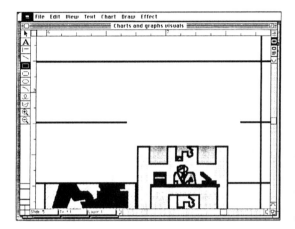

Sometimes, the "trimmer boxes" obscure the background grid. When this happens...

If this occurs, use Persuasion's perpendicular line drawing tool to cover the box, restoring the integrity of the grid. Use the "Line type" from the Effects menu to match the line thickness used in the chart. Notice how easily the line snaps into proper position (as long as you haven't selected "Grid snap off").

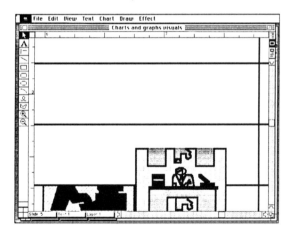

...redraw the grid by using Persuasion's line drawing tool.

The final step is to use Persuasion's Text tool to add a new identifying legend. Be sure to provide a key to help scale the images.

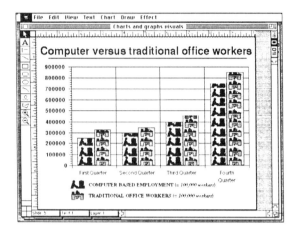

You can choose to use the original columns behind the "Art of Persuasion" illustrations...

Options

Many possibilities remain, limited only by your imagination and good taste.

- Using Persuasion's "Layering" command, you could use builds. These could be especially effective used in electronic presentations if the clip-art images appeared on the screen from the bottom up of each column (using Persuasion's Wipe up Transition effect between layers).

- By clicking on "Show value label" from the Chart menu, you could add the exact figure to the top of each chart—modified, if necessary, as described in the beginning of this chapter.

You could also eliminate the columns of the chart, by double-clicking on each series and choosing a line pattern and fill pattern similar to the Slide master background, allowing only the clip-art to remain.

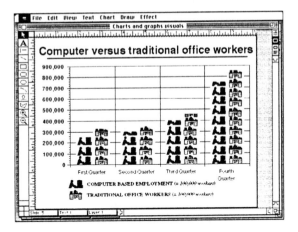

...or you can eliminate the columns, leaving the illustrations to tell their story on their own!

HELPFUL HINT

After double-clicking on the columns to change their line and fill colors, you have to click on the chart and use Persuasion's "Send—To back" command, since selecting an object brings it to the top layer. Otherwise, the chart will hide the clip-art.

The above just scratches the surface of the creative possibilities Persuasion offers you—especially in color. By experimenting with the tools found in the Chart, Draw and Effects menu, you will undoubtedly find new ways to create exciting information graphics using the "Art of Persuasion" clip-art included.

ADVANCED TECHNIQUES CHECKLIST

1) Have I used Persuasion's ungroup feature to increase text legibility—including value labels and information located along the X- and Y-axes of my charts?

   _____

2) Have I experimented with different fill patterns—including graduated screens—for the various elements of my charts?

   _____

3) Have I chosen column fill colors which neither "fight" nor blend into Slide master backgrounds?

   _____

4) Have I exercised restraint, using Persuasion's Draw and Effect tools to inform rather than attempt to impress?

   _____

5) Did I fine-tune my chart by replacing grid lines which may be inadvertently covered by boxes used to trim clip-art images at the tops of columns?

   _____

6) Have I included a legend which clearly identifies all parts of the chart?

   _____

Use this worksheet to make sure that you have used all of Persuasion's abilities to add interest to charts and graphs.

Review and looking forward...

This chapter concludes a survey of the steps involved in preparing the "content" portion of your presentation.

The next two steps include reorganizing your presentation so that slides follow each other in a logical order and preparing speaker's notes and audience handouts.

Then, all that remains is to produce and deliver your presentation!

Chapter Eight:
Reorganizing and reformatting your presentations

After you have created your slides and overheads, review your presentation from your audience's point of view using Persuasion's Slide Show feature. As you review it, you'll probably feel that some slides and overheads are out of order. Persuasion's Slide sorter view makes it easy to reorganize them into the proper order. The Slide sorter view also allows another opportunity for you to apply Slide masters.

Persuasion's Slide sorter and Slide show features are just two more ways Aldus Persuasion goes beyond desktop publishing programs. Using Persuasion's Slide show feature, you can easily preview your presentation as if you were sitting in the audience. Each slide or overhead—including builds—will appear on the screen of your computer either automatically at timed intervals or whenever you click the mouse button. Persuasion's Slide show feature will give you an entirely new perspective on your presentation.

If changes are indicated, they will be immediately obvious when viewing a Slide show. For example, if you discover that the sequence of some of slides or overheads should be changed, Persuasion's Slide sorter view makes it easy to change the sequence of your slides.

You can also use the Slide sorter view to reformat slides, applying new Slide masters.

Using the Slide show feature

At any time, you can review your presentation by clicking on Slide show under the File menu. You'll also use the "Slide show" feature for computer-based on-screen presentations, as described in Chapter Ten.

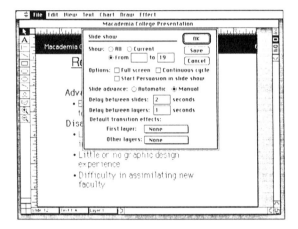

The "Slide show" dialog box allows you to specify the range of slides to be displayed.

The "Slide show" dialog box allows you to preview your entire presentation or a just range of slides. Other options include:

- "Full screen," which produces a larger image
- "Continuous cycle," which repeats the slide show after it has been completed.

HELPFUL HINT

Choose "Current" if you want to check for proper development of builds created on different layers of the individual slide you're working on at the present time.

Slides can advance either automatically or one at a time. In the automatic mode, you can specify the number of seconds between the introduction of slides as well as the speed with which layers of a build are introduced.

HELPFUL HINT

Choose "Manual" if you are producing a computer-based, on-screen presentation. Slides and builds will change each time you click on the mouse button.

To end an automatic presentation, use the Escape key or the Command "." keyboard shortcut which is also used to stop printing.

Working with Persuasion's Slide sorter view

Persuasion's Slide sorter view permits you to view all of your slides or overheads at reduced size, side-by-side on the screen of your computer. You can view your presentation as a whole and check for proper slide sequence. It also makes it easy to re-arrange slide sequence.

Enter Persuasion's Slide sorter view by selecting "Slide sorter" under the View menu.

Choosing appropriate image size

A new menu appears when you choose Slide sorter view.

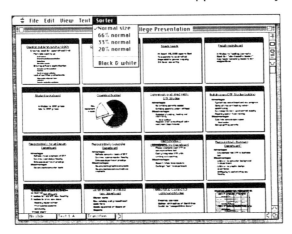

Choosing "Actual size" displays the most slides in Persuasion's Sorter view.

The sorter menu allows you to specify the size of the slides. You can show more slides as you reduce the number of slides on the screen. When you choose "Actual size" or "66% normal," fewer slides can fit on the screen—although more text will be readable and more detail will be visible.

If you are working on a Macintosh II with a color monitor, the "Black and white" option can significantly speed up your work. By disabling color, your screen will be redrawn much faster whenever you move a slide.

HELPFUL HINT

Get in the habit of turning color off as you work in Slide sorter view. It will permit you to work faster.

Moving individual slides

To move a slide from one position to another, start by clicking on it. When the eight handles appear, grab it by clicking anywhere inside the slide and holding down the mouse button.

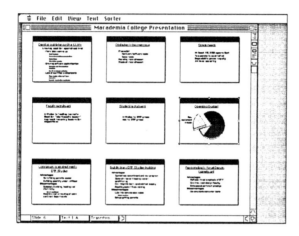

The dots surrounding the slide containing the graph indicate that it has been selected for movement.

Observe the black bar that appears and disappears as you move the slide around the screen. The black bar indicates the location where the slide will be placed when you release the mouse button.

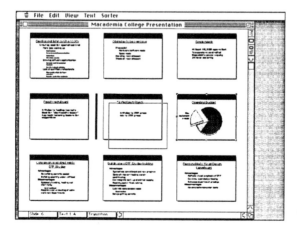

The black bar indicates where the slide will be repositioned if you release the mouse button.

Release the mouse button when the black bar appears between the two slides where you want it, or at the beginning or end of a row. Instantly, the hole left where the slide was originally placed will be filled and the other slides will re-arrange themselves.

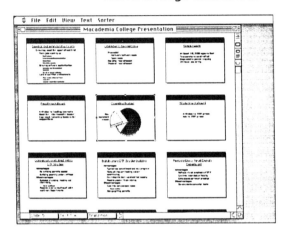

Slide after it has been repositioned, (compare with Page 299).

At the same time, notes and handout sheets will be moved and—where necessary—renumbered to reflect the changed slide location.

Moving multiple slides

You can move more than one slide by holding down the shift key as you select the slides by clicking on them. Note how the slide number at the lower left of the screen changes to "multi-slide" when more than one slide is selected.

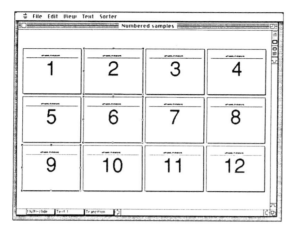

The handles around Slides 2, 6 and 9 indicate they have been selected for movement.

Even if the slides were not originally together in their original locations, they will be grouped together in their new location.

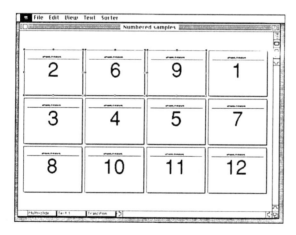

Slides 2, 6 and 9 in their new location.

When selecting multiple slides, to de-select one or more slides after they have been selected—if you change your mind, for example—click again on the slide before you release the Shift key.

HELPFUL HINT

If you want to start all over again, click anywhere on the screen except on a slide. This de-selects all slides. When you do this, notice how the Slide number pop-up menu at the lower left of the screen changes to "no slide."

Applying Slide masters in Sorter view

In addition to re-arranging slide sequence, you can also use the Slide sorter view to change, or apply, Slide masters.

When you click on a slide, the Slide master pop-up menu indicates the Slide master used to format the slide. (If you click on more than one slide, based on different Slide masters, "Multi-Master" will appear in the Slide master pop-up menu.)

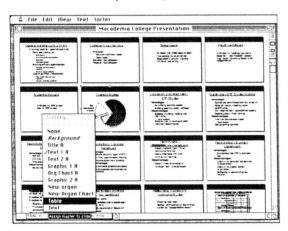

A Slide master can be applied to one, or more, slides selected in the Sorter view.

To re-format your presentation, select one, or more, slides by clicking on them and opening the Slide master pop-up menu. Scroll through the list of available Slide masters and release the mouse button when the desired Slide master is highlighted. Instantly, the slide, or slides, you have selected will be reformatted.

HELPFUL HINT

Remember that the Sorter view does not display builds—only the last layer, or "completed," slide. The only way you can preview builds is by using Persuasion's Slide show feature.

Leaving Sorter view

There are three ways you can leave the Slide sorter view:

- Click on either the Outline, Slide or Handouts icon along the right-hand side of the screen.
- Double-click on the specific slide you want to work on.
- Use the Command key in conjunction with the Left or Right cursor control keys.

As you leave the Slide sorter view, use the following questions to evaluate how effectively your presentation has been organized.

SLIDE SORTER CHECKLIST

1) *Do my slides follow each other in a logical sequence, or do some appear too early or too late?*

2) *Is new information presented in a smooth step-by-step basis?*

3) *Have I used builds to introduce information on complicated slides in a logical way?*

4) *Are there periods in my presentation when too many similar-appearing slides appear?*

5) *Have I avoided abruptly introducing changes in format which disturb the flow of my presentation?*

6) *Have I avoided changes in format not warranted by the contents of the slides or overheads?*

Use these questions as you evaluate your presentation in Persuasion's Slide sorter view.

Review and looking forward...

In the next chapter, we'll look at the final step in producing a presentation—preparing notes and audience handouts. Notes can help you remember important points to discuss or describe in detail as the slides appear.

Audience handouts can magnify the impact of your presentation by adding tangibility and long-life to your ideas. Handouts provide your audience with materials to refer back to as needed. Long after your presentation has ended, your audience can refresh their memories and refer to supporting details.

Chapter ine:

Preparing speaker's notes and audience handouts

You can multiply the effectiveness of your presentation by providing written handouts to those attending. These handouts provide tangible reminders of the important points covered in your presentation. Participants can refer back to important points at a later date as well as review your slides or overheads. Aldus Persuasion also makes it easy to prepare speaker's notes which help you organize and deliver your presentation.

The success of your presentation depends in great measure on the quality of the support materials you prepare. There are two types of support materials: speaker's notes and audience handouts. Indeed, Persuasion's ability to help you prepare these support materials is one of the most important ways it can help your presentation succeed.

Speaker's notes provide the script which you will follow while showing your slides or overheads. They remind you to discuss important points. They provide details which often don't belong on the slides themselves, like explanations of where data originated or how it was compiled.

Most important, placed on the podium in front of you, speaker's notes help you maintain eye contact with your audience while reminding you what each slide or overhead looks like and important points to emphasize.

HELPFUL HINT

It's extremely important that you maintain eye contact with your audience. Each time you glance over your shoulder at the screen or look down at the overhead projector, you lose eye contact with your audience. Speaker's notes set in a large type size help you keep your place in your presentation without breaking eye contact with the audience.

Audience handouts are equally important. These also contain reduced-size versions of your slides and overheads. These take-alongs permit your audience to refer back to your slides or overheads as often as necessary.

Preparing speakers notes

Persuasion Version 2.0, (and following), allows you to prepare speaker's notes while working on the outline of your presentation. This means you can write down the points you want to emphasize as you outline your presentation, while your ideas are still fresh.

An individual speaker's note page is prepared for each slide or overhead. These notes are automatically renumbered and automatically follow your slides and overheads when their sequence is changed.

Formatting speakers notes

Click on the "Notes master" command, located under the View menu. A reduced-size version of the current slide as well as a title placeholder are already placed on the Notes master.

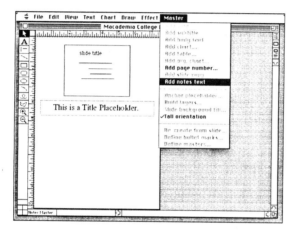

Unformatted Notes master.

You can move or resize the slide thumbnail by clicking on it, using the Selection tool. You might want to make the slide thumbnail smaller, for example, in order to have room for more notes. A smaller thumbnail also permits the use of larger type to refer to during your presentation. Larger type can be read from a longer distance away (so you don't have to put on your glasses or squint at your notes during your presentation).

Another alternative is to click on the title placeholder and move it to the the top of your notes page. When printing your speaker's notes, the title placeholder will be automatically replaced with the title of the individual slide or overhead contained on that page.

To format the title placeholder on your notes pages, choose the text tool by clicking on the large "A" on the left-hand side of your screen, and using the Text tool "I-beam" to highlight "This is a Title Placeholder." Use the various commands located under the Text menu to choose the particular typeface, type size, type style, alignment, line spacing desired for the titles of each page of your notes.

After moving and formatting the title, selecting a large, simple typeface, such as 36-point Helvetica bold, you might want to add a page number to each speaker's notes page. Select "Add page number" from the Master menu . When the double-X symbol appears, you can move it to a desired location on the page and reformat it by highlighting it with the text tool "I-beam" to highlight it and choosing the appropriate commands from the Text menu.

You might also want to use the Text tool to add a status line identifying the presentation and the date of delivery to each page. You can organize presentation and page number information by placing them below a horizontal rule added with the line drawing tool. You can also use the box drawing tool to create a border around each page of your speaker's notes.

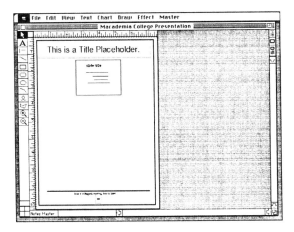

Adding presentation information and a page number to the Notes master.

HELPFUL HINT

Although preparing good-looking speaker's notes might be considered overkill, since you're the only person who will be seeing them, it's important to remember that the success of your presentation is based in large measure on your self-confidence as you deliver it. Thus, anything you do to make yourself feel better about your presentation will be reflected in a more successful presentation!

Placing and formatting the Notes text placeholder

Next, click on "Add notes text" from the Master menu.

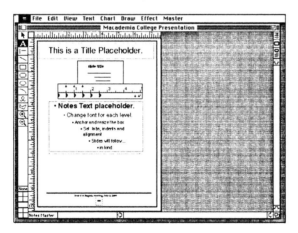

Adding a text placeholder to the Notes page.

The notes text placeholder will appear at the bottom of the notes page. Click on it to move it closer to the title placeholder and slide thumbnail or place it anywhere else on the page.

Next, select the Text tool and drag the "I-beam" through the text notes placeholder to highlight the text. Once again, use the typeface, size, style alignment and line-spacing options to format the test. You can also use the ruler option to adjust tabs and indents. You can also determine whether or not you want to add bullets to your notes.

Notice that if you are preparing your speaker's notes in outline fashion you can use different typeface and type size options for the each level of your notes.

Helpful hint

When formatting speakers notes, use the largest size type practical, bearing in mind that larger type means fewer words can fit on each page. A large, bold-faced sans serif type often is the best best choice. Remember that during your presentation, you're likely to be standing further away from your notes than you are when normally reading a book or newspaper.

Adding notes to your outline

After you have formatted your Notes master, return to Outline view by clicking on the Outline icon, (or use the Command key plus either the Left or Right arrow keys).

As described in Chapter Two, to add speaker notes while outlining:

- Select "Add notes" from the Outline menu, or
- Choose the Command M keyboard command shortcut

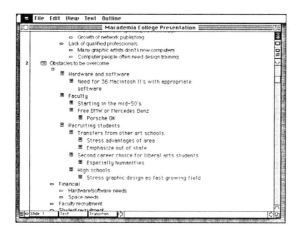

Adding notes to individual subhead levels in the Outline view.

Type your ideas as they appear to you. You can use the same "Text left" and "Text right" commands—or the Backspace/Delete and Tab keys— as you use while outlining. This permits you to visually separate the main ideas you want to emphasize from supporting details.

Previewing your notes

As you add notes in the Outline view, your words will automatically be added to your speaker's notes page which accompanies each slide. Remember that Persuasion will automatically renumber and reorganize your notes pages if you reorganize slide sequence in the Slide sorter or Outline views. Your notes will automatically "follow" your slides, regardless of how often you reorganize your presentation.

There are three ways to preview your notes pages as you're adding notes in Persuasion's Outline view:

- Click on the Notes icon at the right-hand side of your screen—the bottom icon.

- Hold down the Command key while pressing the Left or Right arrow keys which toggles you through Persuasion's various views

- With your mouse, open the View menu and click on "Notes 2," or the number of the notes which corresponds to the outline number you're working on.

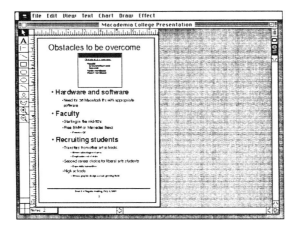

Previewing the notes page with formatted text—compare to Outline view shown on Page 313.

Hiding notes from your outline

Your Outline view on the screen of your computer may quickly become filled up with not only the content of your slides, but your speaker's notes. To hide your speaker's notes, providing you with an uncluttered view of the outline of your presentation, you can either:

- Select "Hide notes" from the Outline menu, or
- Use the Command F keyboard shortcut.

Instantly, your speaker's notes will be hidden.

HELPFUL HINT

You'll probably quickly get in the habit of using the Command F keyboard shortcut to toggle back and forth between revealing and hiding your speaker's notes.

Adding comments to your notes

After creating your notes, you may want to add special comments, such as reminders to emphasize certain points more than others. These can be easily added on individual notes sheets. Start by clicking on the Notes icon. Then, use Persuasion's text and drawing tools to emphasize certain comments or to draw visual connections between parts of the slide and points to emphasize. You'll find the Arrow tool to be a very useful doing this.

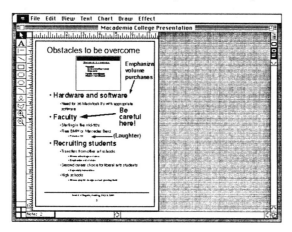

Using Persuasion's drawing tools to enhance a notes page.

Helpful hint

When preparing speakers notes to accompany a computer-based, on-screen presentation, you might want to jot down the number of builds which comprise each layered slide. This will remind you of the number of layers you have to progress through on each slide.

Preparing audience handouts

You can greatly multiply the effectiveness of your presentation by providing thumbnails—or reduced-sized versions of your slides and overheads—to those attending your presentation. Handouts are especially important when using electronic, or computer-based, presentations.

Formatting handouts

Aldus Persuasion makes it easy to prepare audience handouts. The work is done automatically, after you format your handouts pages by selecting the number of slide thumbnails you want to appear on each page and add relevant header and footer information.

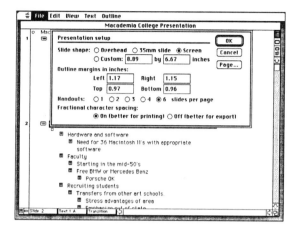

Using the "Presentation setup" box to choose the number of slide thumbnails to appear on each handouts page.

Start by selecting "Page setup..." from the File menu. After verifying printer choice and page size, select "OK." Select whether you want 1, 2, 3, 4, or 6 slides to appear on each page.

HELPFUL HINT

If your presentation is relatively short, or contains a number of detailed charts and graphs, you'll want to have relatively few slides per page, so each can be reproduced larger. If your presentation is primarily text oriented and uses a large type size, you might include more thumbnails on each handout page. In each case, however, make sure that all of the important parts of your message are readable.

Next, select "Handout master" from the View menu. Your previous choice of the number of thumbnails to appear on each page will be reflected in the Handout master. You can now move or resize any of the slide thumbnails by using the Selection tool.

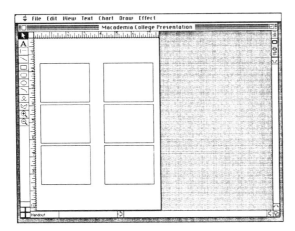

Unformatted Handout master.

With "Handout master" selected, you can also use Persuasion's Text tool to add repeating elements—such as the title, date of your presentation or page number. Be sure to choose a typeface, type size and type style for this information. This information will be automatically added to each handout page.

You can also accent this information with rules, boxes or shadows added with Persuasion's drawing tools.

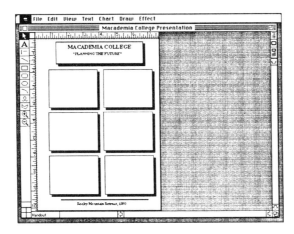

Handout master after repositioning slide thumbnails and adding shadow boxes, presentation information and rules.

To print audience handouts, select "Handouts" from the "Print" dialog box. Note the option which allows you to omit background fills. This option can speeds up printing and can improve the appearance of complicated color slides. Note the "Proof print" option which prints text, but eliminates imported graphics. This feature speeds-up printing test copies of your handouts.

HELPFUL HINT

As described in Chapter Two, you can also print copies of your presentation Outlines for distribution to your audience. If you do, however, be sure you select the "Hide notes" option in the "Print" dialog box, so speaker's notes are not included in the handouts distributed to your audience.

Use the following list to double-check that you have made the most effective use of Persuasion's notes and handouts features.

NOTES AND HANDOUTS CHECKLIST

1) Are your speaker's notes printed in a large, easy-to-read typeface which you can comfortably read while glancing at them from a longer-than-normal viewing distance?

2) Did you limit your speaker's notes to important points or supporting details?

3) Did you use arrows or other visual cues to help you relate important ideas to the material presented in your slides or overheads?

4) Do your notes remind you of presentation details, like the number of builds present on each slide, so you can maintain audience eye contact and not have to keep glancing over your shoulder at the screen?

5) Will your audience be able to easily read the text and understand the visuals included on the slide thumbnails included on audience handouts?

6) Have you included all necessary presentation information on the audience handouts?

Ask yourself these questions as you review the notes and handouts you have prepared to accompany your presentation.

Review and looking forward...

In the next chapter, we'll take a closer look at the various ways you can present your material. We'll examine the strengths and weaknesses of laser printers, ink-jet printers and on-screen presentations. We'll also look at some of the reformatting issues which may be raised when you change from one output format to another.

Chapter Ten:

Output considerations

It is impossible to separate the content of your presentation from the technology which will be used to present it. How you are going to output your Persuasion files inevitably has an effect upon the typeface choices available to you as well as the graphic files you can include in your slides and overheads. Output technology also influences the amount of time it will take to prepare your presentation and complicates switches from format to format.

In Chapter Two, "Planning your presentation strategy," we discussed some of the factors which should influence your choice of presentation media: slides, overheads, flip charts or computer-based on-screen presentations. In this chapter, we take a closer look at putting these alternatives to work.

This chapter introduces one of the significant differences between desktop publishing and desktop presentations. In desktop publishing, most output devices are "transparent." The size of your publication remains the same regardless whether you are printing it on a 300 dot-per-inch Apple LaserWriter or a 1,270 or 2,540 dot-per-inch Lintronic. Headlines and graphic images remain the same size.

When preparing 35mm slides and overhead transparencies using Persuasion, however, the output device you choose influences the size of your working area. For example, 35mm slides are different shapes than overhead transparencies. In addition, the print areas of various output devices are different. The print area of a Hewlett-Packard PaintJet is different than an Apple LaserWriter. Likewise, various projection pads and color monitors cover different areas.

These considerations have to be taken into account when setting up your presentation as well as switching between different output devices. This issue is especially important because it is likely that more than one output device will be used to produce your presentation:

- You may use a color printer or an outside service bureau to produce slides and overheads.

- But, you may proof your work, and print Notes, Outlines and Handouts on a PostScript laser printer.

Black and white overheads

Black and white or color overheads can be quickly produced in your office. Black and white overheads offer the most flexibility. If you have a PostScript printer like the Apple LaserWriter II NT or II NTX, you can quickly translate Persuasion files into overheads. The presentation you're working on this morning can be delivered tomorow—or even this afternoon.

There are two ways you can prepare overheads with a PostScript printer like the Apple LaserWriter II NT:

- You can print your overheads on standard paper and then use your office copier—or a local copying service—to transfer them onto special transparency film.

- Or, you can use special transparency film in your LaserWriter. But, before you do this, make sure that the brand of transparency film you choose is recommended for use in laser printers. The heat involved can cause expensive damage unless you have chosen a brand of transparency film designed for laser printers which won't be damaged by the high temperatures involved.

In either case, overheads can be quickly produced at very low cost.

Apple LaserWriter considerations

In addition to economy, there are several advantages to this approach.

- PostScript printers like the Apple LaserWriter permit you choose from the widest selection of typefaces. You can use any of the hundreds of typefaces available from firms like Adobe Systems, Inc.

- PostScript printers like the Apple LaserWriter permit you to use a wider selection of graphic images and clip art. For example, you can use Encapsulated PostScript (EPS) files created by programs like Adobe Illustrator '88 and Aldus FreeHand.

- You can choose any size type, i.e. 30 point, 31 point, 32 point, 33 point, etc. (As we'll see below, other output devices restrict you to a few major "jumps" in size, i.e. 24 point, 30 point, 36 point, etc.)

Adobe Presentation Pack

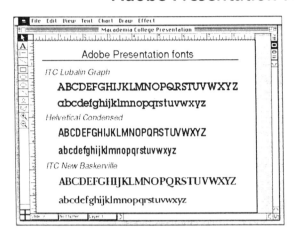

Adobe's Presentations Pack offers a selection of high-legibility typefaces.

Adobe has demonstrated their commitment to the presentations market by creating a special Presentations Package. This package consists of three typeface families chosen specifically for their legibility at long distances. Two serif and one sans serif typefaces are included.

- ITC Lubalin Graph is a serif typeface with a clean, contemporary look. Letters are of uniform thickness and are set wide enough apart to aid easy reading.

- New Baskerville is an elegant serif typeface which works especially well at large sizes. It can add a touch of distinction to your presentations.

- Helvetica Condensed is an extremely useful sans serif typeface. Helvetica Condensed matches the Helvetica typeface built into your PostScript laser printer. Helvetica Condensed's narrow letters and slightly tighter letter spacing permit you to add more words to fit on each line than conventional Helvetica, as the example below indicates. Helvetica Condensed is especially useful for call-out's.

Note the shorter the line-lengths of Helvetica Condensed compared to standard Helvetica.

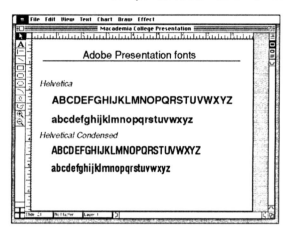

Note the difference in upper and lower case line length between Helvetica and Helvetica Condensed.

Another advantage of preparing overheads on an Apple LaserWriter is that you can include examples created using desktop publishing programs like Aldus PageMaker files saved as Encapsulated PostScript files. These examples can be imported as graphics and enhanced by call-out's (short phrases emphasized by lines and arrows).

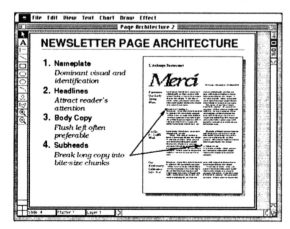

Using call-out's to draw attention to portions of an imported PageMaker file.

The primary disadvantage of creating overheads with Apple LaserWriters is that you are limited to black and white reproduction. You can, of course, enhance them using transparent colored tapes, or—if you are careful—felt-tip pens to add colored borders.In addition, screened backgrounds often have a "granular" effect which becomes magnified when projected.

When printing on the LaserWriter, notice that the LaserWriter dialog box allows you to increase or decrease image area. If you are going to be presenting your overheads in a variety of locations where you don't have total control over screen size, you might experiment with printing your overheads at 85 per cent actual size and—when copying your laser printed originals onto transparency film, place the image at the top of the screen. This is especially important when preparing tall overheads.

HELPFUL HINT

Always place projected images as high on the screen as possible. This helps ensure that everyone in the audience will be able to see the image. Often, if you use the full vertical image area, people in the back of the room will be unable to see information placed at the bottom of the screen.

3M Flip Frame Transparency Protectors

There are three problems which sometimes occur when working with black and white transparencies. One is static electricity which frequently tends to make the transparencies stick together. This forces you to peel them apart while standing in front of the audience, which can interrupt the flow of your presentation. The other problem is how slippery they can be (if static electricity is not present.) Because they are so slippery, they can be easily dropped at the last minute.

In addition, some brands of transparency film used on some office copiers begin to chip after a few presentations. The tiny imperfections become very large when projected on the screen!

One cure for these problems is to place transparencies in 3M RS 7110 Flip Frame Transparency Protectors, (previous numbers 3M 9075 and Scotch 8809). These are ultra-clear transparency holders which not only protect your transparencies but help you keep them organized. 3M's RS-7110 Flip Frame Transparency Protectors are designed to be placed in standard 3-ring binders. This not only protects your transparencies when they're not being used, but makes it easy to safely carry them to and from your presentation.

A final advantage of the 3M Transparency Protectors is that they contain removable flaps which can be used to jot-down ideas which you'll want to mention during your presentation.

Color overheads

There are three ways you can create color overheads:

- Printers like those available from Hewlett-Packard and Tektronix, such as the Hewlett-Packard PaintJet or PaintJet XL

- Color PostScript printers like those available from QMS

- Service-bureau color overheads

The advantages of color overheads is that your presentation avoids a dull, monochromatic impression. Charts and graphs gain tremendous impact when presented in color.

Hewlett-Packard PaintJet and PaintJet XL

The Hewlett-Packard PaintJet is an amazing technological achievement. The PaintJet is an affordable color inkjet printer which, when used with the Hewlett Packard Color PrintKit for Macintosh Computers can produce up to 16.8 million colors when used with Macintosh II computers with color monitors as well as the 8 standard colors when used with a Macintosh Plus or SE. The Hewlett-Packard PaintJet uses a special ink-jet technology which sprays the colors on the special Hewlett-Packard PaintJet Transparency Film. Resolution is 180 dots-per-inch. Additional advantages offered by Hewlett-Packard PaintJets include:

- When used with the Hewlett-Packard fonts supplied, or the Adobe Type Manager, you can safely choose any type size for your presentation: 31 point, 32 point, 33 point, etc.

- The HP PaintJet Transparency Film comes complete with transparent protective sleeves which, like the 3M RS-7110's, are three-hole punched for convenient storage in 3-ring binders.

The Hewlett-Packard PaintJet XL is a faster version of the PaintJet. It prints almost three times as fast.

Although color saturation is not as sharp as available from projected 35mm slides, the Hewlett-Packard PaintJet is capable of preparing highly-detailed, color-saturated overhead transparencies. Because it is an office printer, you have immediate access to your overheads: your color overheads are available for immediate use.

*H*ELPFUL *HINT*

Always maintain an adequate inventory of PaintJet supplies on hand, to avoid running out of ink while printing a presentation. Overnight shipping from Hewlett-Packard Direct, (1-800-538-8787), is available, however.

There are a few disadvantages associated with the Hewlett-Packard PaintJet, however.

- Because the PaintJet is not a PostScript printer, you cannot reproduce Encapsulated PostScript files. You are limited to PICT and PICT2 graphic files created with programs like Claris MacDraw II.

- Printing time and supply costs can be high, especially if you are using color-saturated backgrounds.

The Hewlett-Packard PaintJet is at its best printing solid blocks of color. It is somewhat less successful printing smooth transitions between shades, like graduated fountain effects.

*H*ELPFUL *HINT*

Use the Hewlett-Packard PaintJet to print simple, bold charts and graphs containing large areas of single colors, rather than background fills containing gradual transitions between colors.

Adobe Type Manager

The Adobe Type Manager greatly extends the flexibility of the Hewlett-Packard PaintJet and PaintJet XL. Adobe PostScript typefaces printed with the Hewlett-Packard PaintJet and PaintJet XL are normally characterized by jagged edges. For this reason, the HP Color PrintKit for Macintosh Computers includes a set of scalable Outline fonts which resemble the original Helvetica and Times Roman and Symbol sets. These are high-quality typefaces which can be used at any size between 6 and 250 points.

The Adobe Type Manager, however, allows you to use Times Roman and Helvetica built into the original Apple LaserWriter *as well as any downloadable Adobe typefaces you may have added to your Macintosh.*

The Adobe Type Manager Plus Pack goes even further, and includes the fonts necessary for full compatibility with the LaserWriter Plus and LaserWriter II NT and II NTX. The Plus Pack includes Palatino, Bookman, Avant Garde, New Century Schoolbook, Zapf Chancery, Helvetica Narrow and ITC Zapf Dingbats. (See samples in Chapter Four.)

Because they offer so much typeface versatility, the The Adobe Type Manager and Plus Pack are highly recommended for use with the Hewlett Packard PaintJets.

Using the Hewlett-Packard PaintJet

As is the first step when creating any presentation, the first step is to use the Apple Chooser to select either the Hewlett-Packard PaintJet or the PaintJet XL drivers. (Notice how the shapes of the icon resemble the printers themselves.) In addition, before you can use either PaintJet, you have to disable the AppleTalk network. Notice, also, that you have to specify the port where the PaintJet is connected.

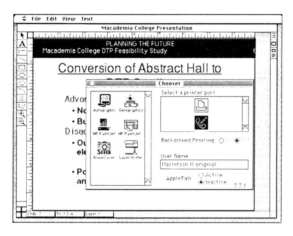

Choosing the Hewlett-Packard PaintJet.

The second step is to choose the appropriate page setup. This determines the size of the transparency you'll be creating and whether it will be horizontally or vertically orientated. When switching from an Apple LaserWriter to the PaintJet, you will be prompted to confirm that the page set up matches the PaintJet's image area before you can continue printing.

After creating your presentation, select the "Print" dialog box. Be sure to select only the options you want to print. Accordingly, deselect "Outline," "Handouts" and "Notes."

If you are only going to print part of your presentation, enter the numbers of the slides you want to print.

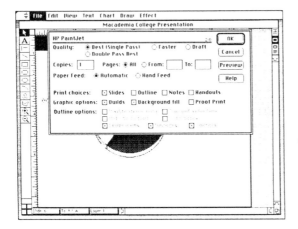

Choosing which portions of your presentation you want to print in the "Hewlett-Packard PaintJet print" dialog box. Be sure to deselect portions you don't want to print.)

HELPFUL HINT

Before printing, get in the habit of always double-checking the print options you have selected. Make sure that you only print that portion of the presentation—slides, notes, handouts or outline—that you desire. Otherwise, you'll end up printing color notes, handouts and outlines when you only wanted black and white copies.

Next, preview your presentation by clicking the "Preview" option. The Hewlett-Packard Color PrintKit software contains a preview feature which helps you avoid expensive mistakes. You can advance through the presentation by clicking on the Left/Right arrow icons at the bottom left of the screen. You can also increase the size of the preview image, to double-check portions of an overhead at increased magnification, by clicking on one of the "mountain" icons in the center of the screen.

Using the Hewlett-Packard PaintJet's Preview feature. (The image is displayed in color on color monitors, of course.)

When you are satisfied that all is well, click on "Print" and the PaintJet will guide you through inserting the transparency pages into the printer.

HELPFUL HINT

After using the PaintJet, before printing your outline, handouts and notes pages, use the Chooser to return to your LaserWriter printer and make sure you turn the AppleTalk network back on. Once again, be sure you make the correct selections in the "Print" dialog box.

Color PostScript printers

Several color PostScript printers have appeared from firms like QMS and Tektronix and more are on the way. Both ink-jet and thermal models are available. These cost significantly more than printers like the Hewlett-Packard PaintJets, but provide you with the ability to incorporate more sophisticated graphics and Encapsulated PostScript files into your overheads. These often offer more sophisticated color effects, including smoother transitions between colors.

Because of their cost, however, you probably have to be in a high volume environment to justify their cost (unless their cost can also be justified by performing other color printing chores—i.e. preparing color proofs of PageMaker-prepared advertisements, brochures and newsletters).

Service bureau transparencies

Service bureaus like Genigraphics can also prepare color transparencies. These offer the most flexibility and the highest possible color quality. In addition, when the transparencies are returned to you, they will be mounted in sturdy cardboard mounts.

In addition to a significant quality advantage, color transparencies prepared by firms like Autographix, Genigraphics and others offer another major advantage: economy. You only have to pay for the transparencies that you use, as you need them. You do not have to make a major capital investment nor buy supplies (which may be hard to locate in your area).

There are two ways you can communicate with service bureaus like Autographix and Genigraphics:

- You can physically deliver your Persuasion files to them via mail courier or overnight express service.
- If you have a modem attached to your computer, you can transmit your Persuasion files using your telephone lines.

Since color transparencies are produced the same way as 35mm color slides, the procedures involved in working with Autographix and Genigraphics will be described in greater detail in the next section.

35mm Slides

There are two ways to create color slides from Persuasion files:

- You can use a film recorder, like the Presentation Technologies FR-1, connected to your computer.

- You can transmit your Persuasion files to service bureaus like Autographix or Genigraphics using either a modem or courier service.

Your choice should be primarily determined by the number of slides you prepare each year, although there are some quality differences between the options.

Film recorders

At first glance, film recorders appear to offer the most convenience. After all, film recorders are located in your office where they can be used at your convenience. However, there are a few problems associated with them:

- Film recorders take a lot of time to operate. In most cases, they should be used with a dedicated Macintosh II, as they tie up your computer for long periods of time while processing slides.

- Unless you have your own color photographic darkroom, the film will have to be sent out for developing and mounting in slide carriers after you have created your slides.

- Because film recorders are typically not PostScript devices, you are again limited in the number of typefaces and graphic file formats which can be used with them. Most include their own down-loadable typefaces which occupy additional hard-disk space.

Film recorders are also expensive—equalling, in most cases—the cost of a Macintosh computer equipped with a color monitor.

It also might take you a certain amount of time to get quality results from a film recorder. You might have to experiment with film types and development options to get exactly the results you're after.

For these reasons, film recorders make the most sense in high-volume applications where numerous slides are going to be produced each month.

Service bureaus

For most individuals, service bureaus like Genigraphics and Autographix make the most sense.

There are several advantages to using outside service bureaus like Autographix or Genigraphics:

- Your computer is not tied up processing the slides. You can be working on another project while your slides are being produced.

- Slides come back developed and mounted under dedicated conditions. Instead of a sideline, these firms specialize in developing and mounting slides.

- Autographix and Genigraphics offer fast, flexible service through a nationwide network of facilities located in major cities. Normal turnaround time is forty-eight hours, although twenty-four hour and same day rush service is also available.

- Both Autographix and Genigraphics offer special incentives to start using their software and services. (Information is included with Persuasion's packaging.)

Both Genigraphics and Autographix have recently opened facilities in Nashville, Tennessee. These Nashville locations virtually guarantee next-day delivery anywhere in the United States via Federal Express. Nashville is the hub of Federal Express—it's where shipments from throughout the country are sorted in the middle of the night before continuing on to their destination.

There is also a quality advantage. Because they specialize in slide production, Autographix and Genigraphics use the most sophisticated equipment available. Autographix and Genigraphics have invested many hundreds of thousands of dollars worth of state-of-the-art equipment in their production facilities. This investment in constantly-updated state-of-the-art equipment pays off in terms of:

- Far better color saturation.
- More accurate color reproduction, including smooth transitions between colors.
- Higher resolution—or slide detail. (You can see the difference in slides containing intricate graphics or scanned images.)

Preparing an Autographix or Genigraphics or presentation

The starting point for preparing a slide or overhead presentation for production by Autographix or Genigraphics is to open the Apple Chooser and select either the Autographix or Genigraphics driver.

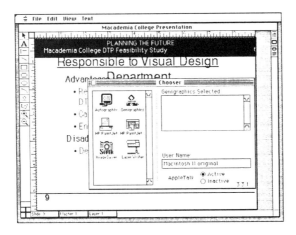

Using the Chooser to select the Genigraphics driver.

After choosing the appropriate driver, select "Page setup" from the File menu. In most cases, choose the top, or "Genigraphics" option. The "4 by 5" and "7 by 9" film formats are there for specialized applications—like preparing rear-illuminated transparencies for trade shows.

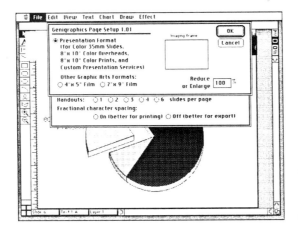

Choosing the proper Genigraphics presentation format.

Next, in the "Presentation setup" dialog box, choose whether you want to produce slides or overheads.

Notice how the length and width dimensions change when you select between 35mm slides and overheads. This is because 35mm slides are wider than overhead transparencies. (35mm slides resemble a 2:3 ratio, overheads are closer to a 4:5 ratio.)

At the Chooser level, you may notice a major difference between the Autographix and Genigraphics production services. Autographix offers you a bit more flexibility. As shown below, the "Autographix page setup" box allows you to prepare either portrait or landscape slides and overheads:

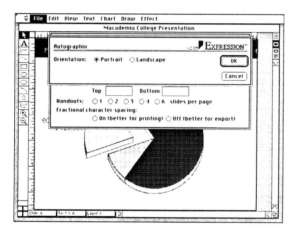

The Autographix driver allows you to create either portrait or landscape slides and overheads.

- Portrait slides and overheads are designed for vertical projection—they're tall and skinny.

- Landscape slides and overheads are designed for horizontal projection—they're wider than they're tall.

Creative considerations

When preparing presentations which Autographix or Genigraphics will produce, it is extremely important that you limit your typeface choices to those typefaces which are built into the Apple LaserWriter Plus, or LaserWriter ll NT series. These include plain, bold, bold italic and italic versions of:

- Avant Garde
- Bookman
- Courier
- Helvetica
- Helvetica Narrow
- New Century Schoolbook
- Palatino
- Symbol (plain only)
- Times
- Zapf Chancery (plain only)
- Zapf Dingbats (plain only)

You may want to refer back to Chapter Four to review these options. Note that the Symbol, Zapf Chancery and Zapf Dingbats typefaces do not include bold, bold italics or italics style options.

In addition, you should limit your choice of type sizes to those which are present on Persuasion's Screen fonts diskette. This means you should avoid sizes that are not included as bold-faced or outlined alternatives on the "Size" submenu located in the Text menu.

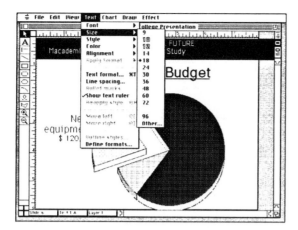

When sending slides and overheads to Genigraphics or Autographix, be sure you limit your type size options to those listed in the "Size" dialog box.

If you choose "other" and enter a non-standard type size, there is a good chance that you may run into problems with line-endings. Lines that appear to be properly sized on the screen of your computer may extend off the side of the slide or overhead when it is printed.

Although, as described below, you will be warned when saving the Autographix or Genigraphics files that they contain inappropriate typefaces and/or type sizes, and you sometimes can get by with using them, doing so is an example of unnecessarily asking for trouble.

Saving files

After creating your presentation, choose the "Print" option. The "Genigraphic print" dialog box prompts you for the quantities of slides and overheads required as well as shipping information. You can specify whether you will be sending your files to Genigraphics via modem or diskette, and how you want your presentation returned to you. You can also specify whether or not you want individual slides and overheads produced for builds.

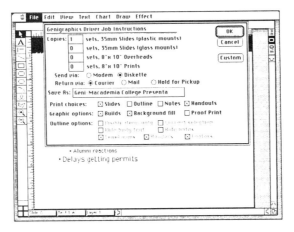

Be sure you select only those portions of your presentation you want Genigraphics to prepare. Notice that "Handouts" is mistakenly selected.

If you are saving your Genigraphics file to diskette, the next dialog box allows you to specify the folder and/or disk drive where you want the file stored. In order to keep presentations saved in the Genigraphics (or Autographix) formats separate from copies of the presentations designed for printing on laser printers, create a special Genigraphics Autographix) folder in your system folder.

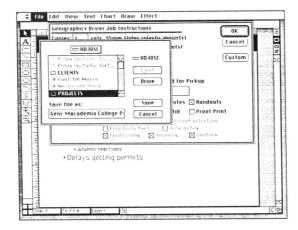

Selecting the folder where you want to store Persuasion files in Genigraphics format.

You have to be extremely careful when saving a Genigraphics or Autographix file. Persuasion remembers the last print command used. Handouts were last printed in the example below—notice that "Handouts" is the only option chosen. Unless this error were noted, you would end up with Genigraphics-produced color handouts but no slides!

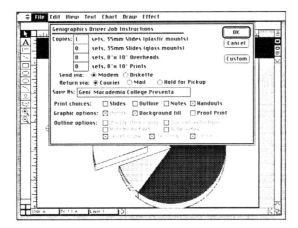

Mistakenly sending handouts to Genigraphics via modem for return!

HELPFUL HINT

When you save an Autographix or Genigraphics file to disk, make sure that "Slides" is the only option selected!

While saving your file, Genigraphics will stop and inform you of any potential problems. You are informed not only of the problems, but—as an added convenience—which slides contain them. Typical examples include:

- Graphic images too large to fit in slide or overhead area
- Unsupported typefaces
- Unsupported type sizes or type styles
- Unsupported graphic file formats

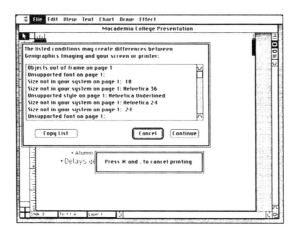

Genigraphics error list.

For your convenience, this list can be copied and printed out for reference while modifying your presentation.

After you have been informed of any possible problems, Genigraphics proceeds to the "Billing Information" dialog box. This allows you to specify different billing and shipping addresses. The "Billing Information" dialog box also offers several payment options. You can choose between the major credit cards, C.O.D. or a previously-established Genigraphics account.

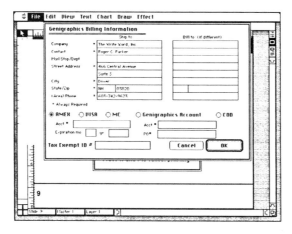

The "Genigraphics billing" dialog box allows for separate shipping and billing addresses.

Close your presentation and quit Persuasion after saving your file. Genigraphics will have saved your file with the "Geni" prefix ahead of it, so it can be immediately identified as a different file from versions saved for printing with an Apple LaserWriter or Hewlett-Packard PaintJet.

Previewing your Genigraphics presentation

Genigraphics includes GeniPeek, a software program which allows you to preview previously-saved Genigraphics files. After closing Persuasion, click on the GeniPeek program icon. When loaded, select "Open" from the File menu. Scroll through your folders until the file with the "Geni" prefix is located.

GeniPeek options located in the View menu include a choice of "Actual Size" or "Sized To Fit." By selecting "Slide," you can scroll through the list of available slides and preview each one.

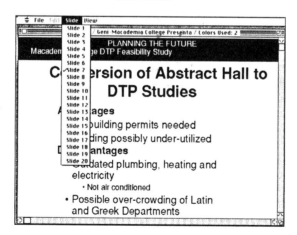

Using GeniPeek to preview your slides.

The GeniPeek program offers another advantage: as you can see from the top right of the screen, it informs you of the numbers of colors used in your presentation. Although you can choose between 16.8 million colors, this doesn't mean they can all be used in a single slide! You are typically limited to 256 colors. Although 256 colors may seem like a lot, graduated background fills (like smooth transitions consisting of blue backgrounds fading into yellow), can include hundreds of different shades in themselves. By keeping you informed of the number of colors used in your presentation, GeniPeek prevents you from inadvertently exceeding the 256-color limit.

Transmitting files

Also included in the Genigraphics software is a communications program which makes it easy to send Persuasion files saved in the Genigraphics format—i.e. while the Genigraphics driver was selected with the Apple Chooser. If you have a modem, you'll find the Genigraphics GraphicsLink software program will make it easy to send your presentations across the street—or across the country—for fast, convenient imaging.

HELPFUL HINT

It is important that you store Genigraphics files in a special Genigraphics folder located in your system folder. The GraphicsLink program does not allow you to search through different folders to locate a specific presentation.

The "GeniLink Communications Setup" dialog box allows you to select the location of the the Genigraphics service bureau closest to your office for automatic dialing. In addition, you can select a transmission rate of either 1,200 or 2,400 baud depending on the type of modem you have. (A 2,400 baud modem costs more but saves on long-distance charges).

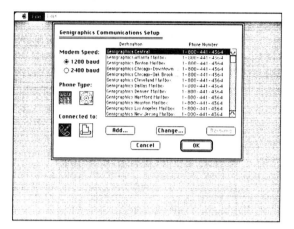

Choosing a Genigraphics location across town, across the country, or in Memphis, Tennessee for next-day delivery.

When selected, the GeniLink program lists the status of all of Genigraphics format files stored in the Genigraphics folder. It also informs you of estimated transmission times. Because long distance rates go down at night, GeniLink allows you to specify a later time for the files to be automatically sent to Genigraphics. Note that more than one file can be selected for transmission immediately, or at a later time.

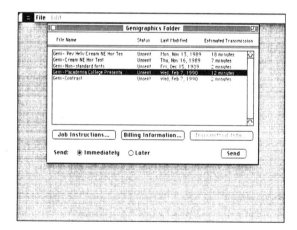

Choosing files for transmission to Genigraphics via modem.

When you select "Send," GeniLink automatically compresses the file so that it will be communicated as quickly as possible, places the call, and sends the file. While the file is being sent, you are kept informed of progress. You can see at a glance how many files have been sent and how many remain to be sent.

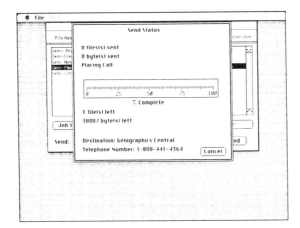

Genigraphics keeps you informed while files are being transmitted.

Working with Autographix

The procedure for working with Autographix is very similar to working with Genigraphics. You start by printing a copy of your presentation to your computer's hard disk, saving all, or just part, of your presentation. As before, it makes sense to store all of your Autographix format files in a single folder, where they can be quickly located.

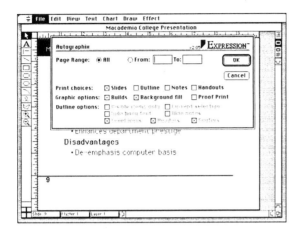

The "Autographix print"
dialog box.

HELPFUL HINT

Once again, when printing presentations to disk with Autographix selected in the Chooser, make sure that only "Slides" and "Builds" are selected!

After saving your presentation in Autographix format, quit Persuasion and open the AGXit! file which prepares your presentation for sending to Autographix via diskette or modem. At a glance, you can see which files are ready to be sent.

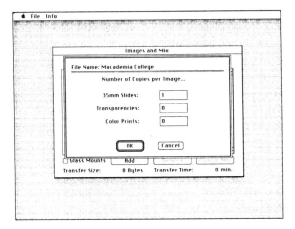

Selecting the number of copies to be made of each image stored in Autographix format...

When adding files to the Autographix transmission folder, you can then specify the number of slides, transparencies and prints you desire.

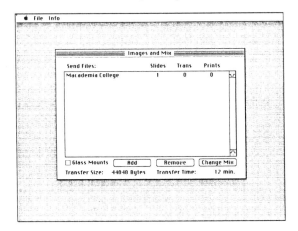

...and deciding between slides, overhead transparencies or prints.

HELPFUL HINT

Be extremely careful when highlighting a file and selecting "Remove." There is no "Undo," so it is possible to inadvertantly remove a file which has not been backed-up. Only the Autographix file, not the original Persuasion file, will be erased, of course.

Then, open the File menu and prepare the files for transmission to Autographix via diskette or modem.

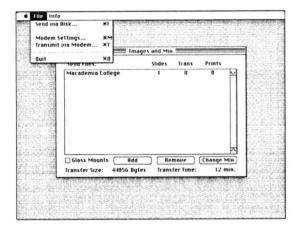

Selecting how your files will be sent to Autographix.

Computer-based presentations

One of the fastest-growing aspects of presentation technology involves computer-based on-screen presentations.

Computer-based presentations are characterized by dazzling special effects—primarily Persuasion's transitions between slides—and a high degree of control over the presentation. Slides and builds can dissolve into each other, or new slides can be revealed by curtains which open from left to right or expose the new slide from top to bottom. In addition, you can advance as slowly or quickly through the slides and builds as desired. In addition, Persuasion 2.0 offers you options like:

- Showing a blank screen or—if desired—a black screen when answering questions or discussing points not covered in the presentation.

- You can emphasize points you're discussing with a mouse-controlled on-screen arrow.

- Keyboard commands allow you to advance through your slides forward or backwards or jump directly to any desired slide.

There are two ways to produce on-screen presentations: projector pads or direct-from screen.

Projector pads

Both black and white and color projector pads are available. These are placed on the tops of overhead projectors, in place of transparencies, and their images are projected onto large, reflective screens. Projector pads allow you to employ sophisticated effects like builds. You can also include dramatic transitions between slides.

The quality of the pad is extremely important, however. The impact of charts and graphs for example, is limited by the sharpness of the screen and the care you take in choosing the grey scales or patterns used to separate the different segments of the charts or graphs. You have to make sure that each element stands our clearly from adjacent segments when projected.

In addition, the sharpness of text is limited by the sharpness of the screen fonts used to reproduce the letters on screen.

Equally important, you have to remember not to include Encapsulated PostScript files or scanned images saved as TIFF files in projected images, since what is displayed is limited to the relatively coarse resolution of the Macintosh screen or projection pad. Reliability issues also have to be faced, if your presentation involves travel.

Before choosing black and white or color a projector pad, make sure that the image it creates is bright enough for the room lighting conditions likely to be encountered and that it is bright enough to project a large, sharp image everyone in the audience will be able to enjoy.

Large screen projection monitors

The new generation of direct-view color monitors is becoming available. These offer greater flexibility. They can be used to display brighter, more color-saturated images and a wider variety of typefaces and graphic file formats.

Although big-screen color monitors are typically used for small audiences, a single computer can be used to drive more than one monitor placed throughout your audience. In addition, large professional audio/video presentation facilities often have permanently-installed video systems which you can connect your computer to.

Regardless whether you're using a black and white projector pad or a high-resolution color monitor, be sure that you create your presentation using the same type of monitor that will be used to display it. You must make sure that the dimensions of the screen used to create your presentation is the same as the dimension of the screen used to display it. Otherwise, there is a likelihood that the tops, bottoms or sides of your images may be clipped off or that an annoying band of bright light may appear along one edge of your images.

HELPFUL HINT

Always create and preview your computer-based presentation on the specific equipment which will be used to deliver your presentation.

Preparing and delivering on-screen presentations

The starting point for an on-screen presentation is to choose "Screen" from the "Page setup" dialog box found in the File menu. The default measurements reflect the size of the monitor being used.

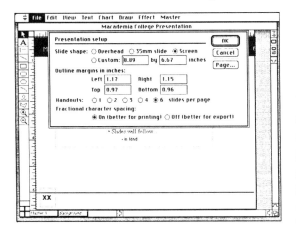

The dimensions of your current screen form the default screen size. If your presentation is going to be presented on a different screen, you must enter different dimensions.

To present an on-screen presentation, select the "Slide show" feature located in the File menu. Notice that, with automatic presentations, you can specify different delays between slides and builds—or individual slide layers. You can increase the size of the image area on your screen by clicking the "Full Screen" option—although to take advantage of this option, the presentation must have been created using an identical screen. Otherwise, the screen might not accommodate the full image area.

To control the transitions between slides, click on the "First layer" Default transition box. This presents you with a list of transitions options. Scroll through the list and release the mouse button when you reach the desired choice. Repeat the process on the box next to "Other layers" to choose the same, or a different, transition effect between layers of individual slides.

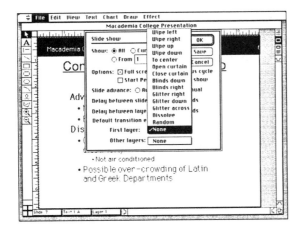

Choosing Slide show transitions between slides and between individual layers of a single slide.

Persuasion 2.0, (and following), offers you several alternative ways of advancing through your slides and builds using a variety of keyboard shortcuts. For example:

To advance to the next slide, or the next layer of a slide:

- Click once on the mouse
- Type the letter N
- Press either the Right or Down arrows
- Type the number 3 while holding down the Command key

To view the previous slide:

- Double-click on the mouse
- Type the letter P
- Press either the Left or Up arrows
- Press the Delete key
- Type the number 2 while holding down the Command key

Holding down the Shift key while performing any of the above "Previous Slide" effects moves you backwards through the layers of a build.

To go immediately to the first layer of the first slide, hold down the Command and shift keys while:

- Pressing the Left arrow
- Typing the letter H
- Typing the number 1

Doing the above while just holding down the Shift key returns you to the last layer of the first slide.

To directly advance to the first layer of the last slide, i.e. before the builds begin, hold down the Command and Shift keys and:

- Press the Right arrow
- Type the number 4

Doing the above without holding down the Command key returns you to the last layer of the last slide, i.e. after the builds have been created.

To go directly to the first layer of a specific slide:

- Hold down the Shift key
- Enter the desired slide number
- Press the Enter, or Return, key

To go directly to the last layer of a selected slide, enter the slide number followed by Return (without holding down the Shift key).

HELPFUL HINT

To return to your original slide sequence, before you jumped to a particular slide, enter the "accent grave"—or backwards apostrophe— key located over the Tab key at the upper left of the Apple keyboard.

Other Slide show keyboard commands include:

- Typing the letter A, or the equals sign, (=), to turn the on-screen arrow—controlled by the mouse— on and off.
- Typing either a B or a comma blanks the screen (turns it white).
- Typing a period turns the screen black.

You can end an on-screen presentation at any time by:

- Typing a hyphen, (-).
- Typing a period while holding down the Command key.
- Typing the letter Q while holding down the Command key.

When using Persuasion's sophisticated transition effects, remember that transitions between color slides place an extra burden on your computer's memory. This is especially true if your slides contain complicated graphics and/or graduated transitions between background colors. In the absence of sufficient memory, there may be a perceptible pause between slides or between layers of a slide.

HELPFUL HINT

Recent advancements like the Adobe Type Manager can improve the quality of on-screen presentations by greatly enhancing typeface quality.

Flip charts

Large flip charts are ideal for presentations in normal room lighting to small groups. Flip charts allow you to use all of the Adobe typefaces plus Encapsulated PostScript files created with Aldus FreeHand and Adobe Illustrator '88.

There are two ways you can prepare flip charts on laser printers.

First, although there are a few laser printers available capable of printing on 11 by 17-inch tabloid-sized pages, most laser printers are limited to an image area of less than 8 1/2 by 11 inches. If you try to print a larger size, Persuasion will automatically tile the images. This means that each page will come out in sections, printed on several sheets of paper which must be glued together.

If you are very careful when you trim the non—printing margins at the edges of each page and aligning the pages, this can result in acceptable results. Often, however, the joints remain obvious. When your presentation exceeds the sizer of the image area prepared by your output device, Persuasion informs you that the images will be tiled.

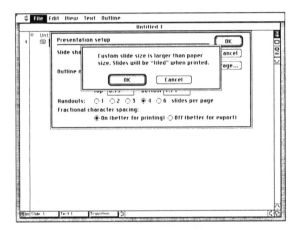

If your flip charts are too large to be printed on a single 8 1/2 by 11 page, each image will be tiled, which means portions will be printed on two, or more, pages.

As an alternative, you can print the image at reduced-size on your LaserWriter using 8 1/2 by 11-inch sheets of paper and then use an office copier with an enlargement feature to create larger flip chart pages.

The disadvantages of enlarging 8 1/2 by 11-inch pages is that the limitations of the 300 dot-per-inch LaserWriter rapidly become obvious when the pages are enlarged. This reduces the sharpness of the letters and visuals included on each page.

Because of these problems, the best way to produce flip charts is to produce them on a high-resolution PostScript output device, like a Linotronic L100 or L 300 phototypesetter. High-resolution phototypesetting replaces the LaserWriter's 300 dot-per-inch output with 1,270 or 2,540 dot-per-inch output. This results in cleaner, crisper letters and smooth graduated backgrounds. Both text and graphics will appear appreciably better.

In addition, high-resolution phototypesetting also eliminates the need to tile your flip chart pages, because high-resolution phototypesetters can prepare pages as tall as desired, either 13 or 17 inches wide, (depending on the specific model used).

High-resolution PostScript phototypesetting is also the ideal choice if your flip charts are going to include graphics created with programs like Adobe Illustrator '88 or Aldus FreeHand. The quality of scanned photographs will also be vastly superior to the quality of scanned photographs reproduced with a 300 dot-per-inch laser printer.

Changing presentation formats

When running "Page setup...," after using the Chooser to select a different output device, Persuasion will prompt you if the new format does not match the previous one. Persuasion will prompt you to go through your presentation and resize text and graphics.

There are several times when you might decide to change presentation formats:

- You might decide to "colorize" an existing presentation by sending black and white overheads originally prepared for printing on an Apple LaserWriter II NT to Autographix or Genigraphics for creation of color transparencies.

- Alternately, you might decide to print black and white overhead transparencies of a presentation originally created as color slides produced by Autographix or Genigraphics.

- Or, as you become more involved with creating color overheads, you might purchase a color printer like one of the Hewlett-Packard PaintJets.

In each case, after selecting a new output device with the Apple Chooser, you have to use the "Page setup..." command to resize your presentation before you can print it. It is best to immediately enter "Page setup..." after selecting a new output device with the Apple Chooser.

Persuasion can automatically re-format your presentation's text and graphics or you can go through your slides and overheads one at a time to make sure they have been properly resized. When reformatting a document, Persuasion 2.0, (and following), offers to do the work for you.

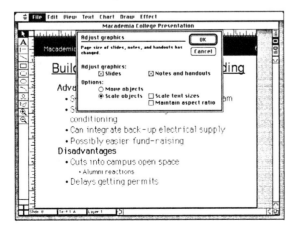

When changing formats, Persuasion can move or resize text and graphic images if desired.

If you want your presentation automatically reformatted, first select whether you want to reformat slides and overheads or notes and handouts.

When you select either alternative, two options become available: "Move objects" and "Scale objects."

- If you select "Move objects," text and graphics will remain the same size, but will be moved to the center of the slide or overhead. This option has to be used with care, however, because large objects may extend beyond the edges of the slide or overhead. Equally distracting, small text and graphics may appear "lost," or "swimming," in the center of your resized presentation.

- If you instead select "Scale objects," Persuasion will automatically resize text and graphics to accommodate the dimensions of your new presentation format or output device.

Choose "Scale text sizes," if you want Persuasion to increase or decrease type sizes in the increments offered under the "Size" option of the Text menu.

Select "Maintain aspect ratio" if you want Persuasion to maintain the height to width ratio of graphics. Otherwise, the shapes of graphics may be distorted, (because slides and overheads have different height to width ratios).

If you simply click on "OK" without making any other selections in the "Adjust graphics" dialog box, it will be up to you to go through each slide and overhead and relocate objects and adjust type and image size.

Helpful hint

When changing presentation formats, always go through each slide and overhead to make sure it has been properly reformatted watching for problems like text or graphics extending off the edge of the slide.

To avoid expensive and frustrating mistakes, use the following checklist before printing your presentation or sending files to an outside service bureau.

PRESENTATION PRODUCTION CHECKLIST

1) Did you avoid including imported graphics files with formats incompatible with the output device chosen?

    _____

2) Did you limit your choice of typeface formats to those supported by the printer or film recorder you will be using to output your presentation?

    _____

3) When preparing files for production by Genigraphics or Autographix, did you limit your typeface choices to those typefaces and type sizes which they specifically support?

    _____

4) When using color printers or film recorders, did you leave sufficient time for printing?

    _____

5) When using a Hewlett-Packard PaintJet or PaintJet XL, do you have sufficient back-up supplies on hand in case the ink reservoirs need to be replaced while printing your presentation?

    _____

6) When producing on-screen presentations, does the computer you will be using contain the Adobe Type Manager to improve typeface resolution?

    _____

                                            (continued)

Ask yourself these last-minute questions before printing your presentation or sending them to an outside service bureau.

7) Before printing your presentation, or sending files out for outside production, did you double-check to make sure that only the desired parts of your presentation have been selected in the "Print" dialog box?

8) When switching between presentation formats, did you adjust the size of text, borders and graphics to accommodate the size of the newly-selected output device?

Checklist continued.

Review and looking forward...

In the final chapter, we'll take a look at what you should do after you have prepared and printed your presentation. We'll look at ways of developing a healthy outlook on your presentation as well as review important things to look for as you set up your room for your presentation.

Chapter **E**leven: Presentation tips

If you've developed your presentation following the six step sequence outlined so far, your presentation is probably in very good shape. At this point, all that remains is to rehearse and polish your presentation, perfecting your timing and paying attention to those little details which spell the difference between "adequate" and "excellent."

If you think you're the only person who has ever been nervous before a presentation, think again. Study after study has shown that fear of public speaking ranks as one of the most common fears. So, if you're still slightly nervous, don't fight it. You're in good company.

This is not to say that you should give in to your nervousness, however. So, accept your anxiety as healthy and normal, but don't let it overwhelm you.

The following are some observations about presentations I've developed during the past two years while travelling around the country delivering a series of presentations ranging in length from less than an hour to a full day. There's nothing scientific about the following, except that the ideas have worked for me.

Presentation attitudes

Have you ever gone to a comedy club and watched a comedian fail? Wasn't it a stressful experience? Didn't you feel uncomfortable watching the comedian fall on his face? Weren't you anxious to see the end of his set? Wouldn't you have rather watched the comedian succeed?

There's an important lesson here: *most audiences want to see you succeed!* Unless you're arguing an unpopular position—that Motherhood and Apple Pie are really bad, for example—most audiences are at least neutral and—at best—predisposed to accept your ideas.

Thus, one of the most important ways you can improve your presentation skills is to constantly remind yourself that *nobody wants to see you fail.* Your audience wants to see you succeed. Nobody wants to be embarrassed by someone else's failure. The audience wants to leave your presentation convinced, excited and motivated. They want to feel that their time, and possibly money, were well spent.

So, constantly remind yourself that the audience is basically on your side. By reminding yourself that the audience is on your side, you can significantly reduce your performance anxiety.

HELPFUL HINT

As you prepare and rehearse your presentation, and as you stand up to begin it, take a few seconds to stop and remind yourself that the audience is on your side.

Next, during your presentation, actively search for positive feedback from the audience.

Choosing audience focal points

One of the best ways to build your confidence as you deliver your presentation is to select a few key individuals as focal points. Maintain eye contact with them and project directly to them. Watch their reactions. These individuals can contribute a great deal to your success.

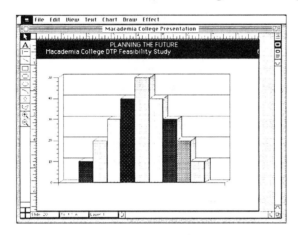

The vast majority of your audience will be on your side, hoping you'll succeed!

Think of your audience as a standard statistical distribution curve with a few people at the ends, but most in the middle. On the "positive" side there will be a few people who will be enthusiastically hanging onto your every word. They'll be nodding their heads in agreement with your every utterance. On the other end of the spectrum, however, there will be a few people who appear to actively disagree with you. They'll be frowning and looking displeased at your every statement.

Most people, however, will be somewhat in the middle.

If you project to the Positives, you will feel better about yourself and—as a result—deliver a strong presentation. By projecting to the Positives, you'll do a better job of convincing the unconvinced—the great majority of the audience who are likely not providing visual clues of agreement or disagreement.

If, however, you allow yourself to be distracted or demoralized by the frowners, you're apt to lose control of your presentation. You're apt to begin worrying that perhaps *everyone* in the audience is unconvinced or in total disagreement with you. You'll begin to lose your enthusiasm and self-confidence—and your presentation will quickly reflect it. Instead of gaining support from those in the middle, you'll lose their support.

With regard to Negatives in the audience, remember that:

- Some people may only appear to be disagreeing with you. They may be frowning because lunch didn't agree with them or they received a speeding ticket on the way to your presentation.

- Frowns may also indicate that the individuals are *paying attention* to you not disagreeing with you.

- Some people may have a vested interest in disagreeing with you. They may be jealous that you're standing up there instead of them or are threatened by your success for other reasons.

No matter what the cause, if you allow the Negatives to derail your presentation, you'll lose the majority of the audience—those in the middle who want to see you succeed.

So, as you prepare to deliver your presentation, identify potential "Positives" in the audience. If possible, try to select individuals who you don't know by name, so you won't be so prone to disregard their support by thinking: "They're only agreeing with me because I'm their boss!" Look for friendly, smiling faces who offer positive reinforcement and accept their support.

Speak from authority

Another technique which I've always found useful is to consciously remind yourself that *you are the expert.* You are standing in front of the room because you have devoted time and energy to gathering information and organizing it in a logical, orderly fashion. Remind yourself that you know more about your subject than those in the audience and that you have developed a point of view which the audience is unaware of. The audience is there because they are at least curious about your conclusions and recommendations.

If you begin your presentation by thinking that the audience knows more about your subject than you do, you are likely to have very little self-confidence. So, take a few minutes to consciously remind yourself that you have developed, to the best of your abilities, an opportunity, solution or unique perspective. The audience wants to hear what you have to say. *You're doing the audience a favor by sharing your ideas and information with them!*

Last minute details

Self-confident presentation skills also come from paying attention to details. Your self-confidence will increase to the extent that you eliminate opportunities for last-minute problems. Your goal is to eliminate potential problems and distractions. Here are some ways you can do this.

Arrive early

If you're delivering a presentation in a distant city, always arrive a day early. Try to visit the presentation room the night before your presentation. The day of your presentation, plan to arrive at least an hour ahead of time.

The last thing you want to do is get lost and arrive at your presentation late or out of breath!

If you have time, check that tables and chairs have been arranged to your satisfaction. Check sight-lines, so that all of your audience will be able to see the screen. If some seats are less desirable than others, try to discourage sitting at them, unless they're absolutely needed. One way to do this is to tilt the chairs forward or put "Reserved" cards on them.

If your presentation is in a hotel or convention center, take a few moments to note the locations of the nearest rest rooms and telephones and announce their location before your presentation begins. This helps show the audience you're a considerate person, interested in their comfort. Try to anticipate questions and be prepared with the answers.

HELPFUL HINT

Don't take it seriously—especially during long presentations—if individuals occasionally get up and leave the room. Many have to check in with the office, etc. (Others may have had too much black coffee.) Try not to allow yourself to be distracted by these interruptions and don't take them personally!

More important, before the audience arrives, run through your slides or overheads one more time. Make sure that the slide projector isaccurately focused. Find out if there is a spare bulb in the room. If you are using overheads, make sure that the image area is properly placed on the screen. Make sure that there is space next to the overhead projector for two stacks of overheads. You'll need one pile for to-be-shown overheads, another for overheads after you have shown them.

Make sure that the table is on the appropriate side of the projector, so you can work from right to left, if that is most comfortable, allowing you to use your most familiar arm. Try to arrange things so that you do not have to block the screen when you switch overheads.

Also, check out the sound system. Make sure that the microphone is connected and that sound levels have been properly set.

HELPFUL HINT

Whenever possible, try to use a clip-on, or lavelier, microphone. These allow you freedom to move around during your presentation rather than being anchored to a podium. Remember that a podium can create a psychological barrier between you and your audience. A clip-on microphone allows you to establish a closer, warmer rapport by approaching the audience. This can be especially important during the opening moments of your presentation when you and your audience are evaluating each other.

A clip-on microphone will also allow you to approach the screen and use a pointer to emphasize various parts of your slides and overheads. (Don't forget that electronic pointers—similar to flashlights—are also available.)

HELPFUL HINT

My perspective has always been that the members of most audiences do not have pleasant memories of their school experiences. As a result, many audiences enter a presentation with the feeling that they're going to be "taught." Accordingly, you'll succeed to the extent that you work with your audience, communicating a feeling that you're there to share knowledge with them, rather than attempting to "teach" them.

The ability to walk around the room and approach the audience can do a lot to breakdown "us" versus "them" feelings.

During your pre-presentation check-out, you should also make sure that the remote control for the slide projector has been hooked up and is performing properly. If the slide projector does not have an automatic focus feature, make sure you know how to operate the focus feature on the remote control. Before your presentation, you'll also want to check out how much wire is available for the slide projector remote control and your clip-on microphone, so you don't inadvertently pull the slide projector off its table or strangle yourself with the microphone cord! (In addition, coil the microphone cord to minimize the possibility of stumbling over it.)

Before your presentation begins, check-out the location of room lighting. You'll want to be able to quickly and easily turn on or off room lighting—or, even better—have someone operate the lights for you. You may be surprised at how confusing room lighting controls are in many hotel conference rooms. Often, switches are located at both the front and back of a room.

Notice that many newer conference rooms allow you to pre-set different lighting levels, so that you can quickly change room lighting levels.

HELPFUL HINT

If you're presentation is being delivered in a hotel or convention center, remember that many establishments do not own audio/video equipment, but merely rent it as needed. This is another reason to check out the equipment the night before, so that there would be enough time for a replacement projector or bulb to be delivered early in the morning, if necessary.

Timing

One of the most important aspects of preparing a presentation is to constantly time it. You want to make sure that it ends on time. Timing is one of the most difficult aspects of presentation development to control.

Only rehearsals can help you decide how much time you will spend with every slide. Try to run through your presentations several times.

One very useful technique is to have some material available which can be added or removed without destroying the continuity of your presentation. For example, you might prepare a few extra overheads which provide an extra level of support to your major conclusion.

If you're familiar with desktop publishing terms, I'm suggesting you have a few "sidebars" available which can be inserted as needed. These would provide a closer look at one or more of aspects your presentation. Likewise, it's an advantage to be able to shorten your presentation by eliminating an overhead or two.

The ability to add or subtract materials during a presentation is an advantage because it is impossible to always be one hundred percent on-time in delivering a presentation.

- You might begin speaking too quickly, which means you might finish too early.

- Or, if there are numerous comments or questions from the audience, you might run out of time.

HELPFUL HINT

One of the least-expensive presentation aids you can purchase is a small, flat, travelling clock. Ideally, the clock should be about two inches square and about an inch thick. It should have large, easily-read hands. (Avoid digital clocks as their read-out's are generally difficult to see in dim light.)

Place this clock face-up behind the podium or behind the overhead projector where you can casually glance down at it. A small clock with big hands allows you to unobtrusively keep track of elapsed time without forcing you to glance at your watch—which inevitably causes everyone in the audience to want to glance at their watches!

Temperature

Temperature can be another distraction. If you're dealing with a large group, be prepared for conflicting comments about room temperature. Be prepared for audiences containing individuals who are both too hot and too cold! If you presentation is primarily based on overheads, be aware that the room is likely to be significantly warmer in the front of the room than the audience. Overhead projectors generate quite a bit of heat.

Audiences will appreciate your concern if you take the time to enquire about their comfort.

Repeat questions

Always repeat questions from the audience. Although you may have been able to understand a participant's question, others in the audience may not have. There are several reasons to repeat questions:

- When you looked at an individual asking a question, you were able to watch their lips as well as hear their words directed at you. Those sitting behind or to the sides of the the questioner did not share your advantage.
- By repeating the question, you can restate it in a simpler, more straightforward way.
- Repeating the question buys you time, so you can begin to prepare your response.

Handouts

Whenever possible, try to get an accurate advance count of the number of individuals attending your presentation so you can prepare an adequate quantity of audience hand-outs. It's always a good idea to bring along a few extra copies.

You'll also want to decide when to distribute your handouts. If you distribute them in advance, the audience may pay more attention to your handouts than your presentation. If you distribute them after your presentation, those who have to leave early—to beat rush hour traffic—may not receive them.

In some cases, you may want to distribute an abbreviated version of the outline as a guide for note-taking, and hand-out copies of your overheads after the presentation.

By saving your best handouts for last, you can end your presentation on a stronger note. Instead of asking for questions—and standing there in embarrassment if no one has any questions—you can take the initiative and state with authority: "OK, in that case, you'll find the handouts in the rear of the room. And thank you."

HELPFUL HINT

Persuasion's ability to prepare both formatted outlines and handouts offers you the opportunity of presenting your audience with an outline containing spaces for them to jot down notes at the beginning of your presentation and detailed handouts containing copies of your slides at the ends of your presentation. This can double the effectiveness of your presentation. Plus, you can use the end of session handouts as a carrot, encouraging everyone to stay until the end.

Ending your presentation

I have always found it useful to end presentations with an emphatic "Thank you!" A strong "Thank You!" signals the audience that your presentation is over. It eliminates a weak, indeterminant ending. Presentations ending with a strong "Thank You" not only show respect for the audience, but generally elicit applause—which is the highest praise any presenter can ever receive!

Backups

You should also determine how many copies of your slides and overheads should be prepared. The temptation is to order or prepare just one set. But, what happens if something happens to it? If you prepare only one set of slides, and it gets lost or stolen on the way to your presentation—or you spill coffee on your only set of overheads—your presentation is off to a very rocky start!

In many cases, the incremental cost of preparing two sets of slides and overheads is just marginally more than preparing one set. As an added precaution, you can take one set with you and a co-worker can bring the other set.

Helpful hint

Needless to say, when travelling by air, always hand-carry your overheads and slides—and it's a good idea to travel wearing clothes which could be worn during your presentation if your luggage got lost.

Always anticipate the worst possible scenario—and plan accordingly! Since so much of the success of your presentation is based on your self-confidence, it's worth a little extra money to prepare a back-up set of slides and overheads.

Last-minute suggestions

I have found it useful to set-up my presentation area ahead of time and then leave the room for a few minutes before the presentation begins. You are likely to find that the most stressful part of your presentation is the fifteen minutes before it starts. Once it starts, if you bear in mind that you know your subject better than the audience and that the audience is on your side, the presentation will proceed smoothly. But, the last few moments are murder!

Accordingly, set up your overheads, place the microphone and remote control where they'll be comfortable, and leave the room. Stretch your legs in the hallway outside the room. If you can, and the weather is co-operating, take a brisk two minute walk around the parking lot. (Make sure that the outside door doesn't lock after you, though!)

HELPFUL HINT

While setting up my presentation materials in the front of the room, I have always found it useful to smile and personally greet a few members of the audience. Even a short "Hello" before the presentation begins is enough to create a "supporter" who will be there when you need it. It's nice to receive a smile or a nod during the beginning moments of a presentation!

At the appointed time, briskly approach the front of the room and welcome the participants. Don't give yourself time to worry! Simply walk to the front of the room, smile and nod at one or two of the people whom you have identified as possible supporters, and begin your presentation.

LAST-MINUTE CHECKLIST

1) Are you planning to arrive at your presentation with enough leeway to accommodate unanticipated last-minute delays?

_____

2) Have you familiarized yourself with the locations of rest rooms, public telephones and controls for room lighting?

_____

3) Have you made sure that overhead and slide projectors are properly hooked-up and focused? Are you with familiar with their operation— especially slide projector remote controls?

_____

4) Is the sound system performing properly?

_____

5) Have you backed-up your slides and overheads and made sure that extra projector bulbs are available?

_____

6) Did you bring enough handouts for everyone likely to attend your presentation—plus a few extras?

_____

7) Did you bring a small clock so you don't have to look at your watch?

_____

8) Have you identified possible supporters in the audience who can boost your self-confidence?

_____

Use these questions to review room setup and your last-minute preparations.

Conclusion

As you have seen, Aldus Persuasion offers you a totally new way of creating and delivering presentations.

Instead of working against you, Aldus Persuasion works with you, helping you organize your ideas and translate them into compelling slides, overheads, flip-charts and on-screen presentations.

All that remains is the fun. Because, that's what presentations should be. Chances are, you're doing what you're doing because you enjoy doing it. Aldus Persuasion makes it easy to share your knowledge and enthusiasm with others.

You already have always accumulated a significant body of knowledge. By making it easy to organize and communicate that knowledge, Aldus Persuasion helps your presentations succeed.

Bibliography

Gronbeck, Bruce E. *The Articulate Person: A Guide to Everyday Public Speaking.* Glenview, IL: Scott Foresman and Company, 1983.
A useful review of the basics of inter-personal communication. Stresses techniques you can use to plan your presentation planning on the basis of audience expectations and likely reactions.

Hoff, Ron. *"I Can See You Naked:" A Fearless Guide to Making Great Presentations.* Kansas City: Andrews and McMeel, 1988.
An entertaining, common-sense look at presentation dynamics. Strong chapters on starting off on the right foot, nervousness and handling audience questions. The emphasis throughout is on building a strong relationship with your audience.

Holmes, Nigel. *The Designers Guide to Creating Charts and Graphs.* Watson-Guptil, 1983.
*A colorful look at the powers—and pitfalls—of information graphics. Numerous color examples will stimulate your own efforts to move beyond charts and graphs into the types of information graphics which make **Time** Magazine and **U.S.A. Today** so entertaining. Written by a pioneer in the field.*

Lambert, Clark. *The Business Presentations Workbook.* Englewood Cliffs, NJ: Prentice-Hall, 1988.
Interactive, step-by-step planning guide containing numerous checklists for you to fill-out while analyzing your audience and your message. Contains checklists for planning new business, marketing, sales training and other specialized presentations. Spiral-bound, 8 1/2 by 11-inch format helps you put the worksheets quickly to work. Several Key Point Summarizer worksheets will help you anticipate and prepare appropriate answers for possible audience questions.

McComb, Gordon. *Executive Guide to PC Presentation Graphics.*
New York: Bantam Books, 1988.
Although oriented to MS-DOS computers, this volume,
nevertheless, offers a handy review of the basic elements of
presentation design and production.

Parker, Roger C. *Looking Good in Print: A Guide to Basic Design*
for Desktop Publishing, 2nd ed. *Chapel Hill: Ventana Press,*
1990.
In addition to a chapter on color, the second edition contains
a chapter devoted to designing good-looking presentation
materials. The expanded Makeover section contains "before"
and "after" examples.

Parker, Roger C. *The Makeover Book: 101 Design Solutions for*
Desktop Publishing. *Chapel Hill: Ventana Press,* 1988.
Chapter 9, "Charts and Graphs," contains several before and
after examples.

Peoples, David A. *Presentations Plus: David Peoples' Proven*
Techniques. *New York: John Wiley & Sons,* 1988.
Concise, organized review of effective presentation planning
and delivery techniques. Peoples' use of frequent checklists
and summaries of both right and wrong presentation charac-
teristics will help you put his techniques immediately to work.

Rabb, Margaret Y. *The Presentation Design Book: Projecting a*
Good Image with Your Desktop Computer. *Chapel Hill:*
Ventana Press, 1990.
*The first non-software-specific design guide to appear, **The***
***Presentation Design Book** offers an in-depth look at the*
elements which contribute to strong presentations. Special
emphasis is placed on making the right color choices.
Presentation planning tools include ready-to-copy storyboards
for slides, overheads and on-screen presentations.

Tufte, Edward R. *The Visual Display of Quantitative Information.*
Cheshire, CT: Graphics Press, 1983.
Required reading for the advanced presenter, especially
*presenters who employ a lot of charts and graphs. **The Visual***
***Display of Quantitative Information** is both an historical look*
at the subject as well as a fountain of useful tips and
techniques.

Wagner, Carlton. *The Wagner Color Response Report.* 1989: *The Wagner Institute for Color Research. 802-682-1143.*
Are you inadvertantly sending the wrong message to your audience? A psychologist specializing in the use of color and its effect on people looks at the emotional properties of each of the primary colors. Colors are analyzed in terms of the "signals" they send. Strongly organized, each chapter ends with a strong summary.

White, Jan V. *Using Charts and Graphs: 1000 Ideas for Visual Persuasion. New York: R. R. Bowker Company, 1984.*
Although written in pre-desktop days, this still remains one of the most practical and useful guides available.

Wohlmuth, Edward. *The Overnight Guide to Public Speaking. Philadelphia: Running Press, 1983.*
Although you can, indeed, read **The Overnight Guide to Public Speaking** *the night before an important presentation, you'll probably want to keep it around as a practical handbook. Each page contains practical advice about room set-up, introducing others—and being introduced.* **The Overnight Guide** *begins with "Ten Sure-Fire Ways To Give A Lousy Speech" and continues in a similar, light-hearted vein. Special emphasis is placed on "The Six Signals All Audiences Want To Hear."*

Index

A

Adobe Presentation Pack, 326-327

Adobe Type Manager, 134, 330, 332

Alignment tool, 261-264

Anchoring text, 173-174

Apple Extended Keyboard, 49

Apple LaserWriter
  Advantages, 325-326
  Printing, 39-43, 325

Area chart, 197

Arrows, 230

Aspect ratio, 247-248

Autographix
  Preparing files, 350-352
  Sending files via modem, 353

AutoTemplates
  Creating, 94-95
  Creating default, 119-120
  Ignoring default, 94
  Modifying, 185-187, 224-225
  Previewing, 84
  Versus Presentations, 95, 118-119
  Working with existing, 85-86

Avant Garde, 129, 130-131

Axes—formatting chart, 209-210

B

Back-up presentation
  materials, 37, 381

Bar chart, 194

Blinds, 21

Bookman, 129, 131-132

Border
  Creating, 102-104
  Options, 77-78

Builds
  Text, 184-186
  Charts, 219-223
  Purpose, 19-20

Bullets, 158-159

C

Callouts
  Adding to chart, 218
  Adding to imported graphic, 327

Centering objects, 259-261

Charts
  Builds, 219-223
  Created with clip-art, 283-291
  Defining formats, 205-206
  Enhancing, 276-282
  Entering data, 212
  Exporting, 223-224
  Formatting, 202-205
  Importing data, 213-214

Reformatting, 217-219
Slide masters, 206-207
Types, 193-201
Checklists
Advanced charting
techniques, 292
Outline, 58
Charts, 225-256
Design, 82
Drawing tool, 273
Notes and handouts, 320
Outline, 72
Presentation format, 38
Presentation setup, 383
Production, 366-367
Slide masters, 120-121
Slide sorter, 304
Typeface selection and use,
187-188
Chooser, 39-40
Circles, 249
Clip-art, 255-259
Collapsing an outline, 59-60
Colors
Attributes, 233
Defining, 238-239
Column charts, 195
Combination charts, 201
Courier, 129, 133

D

Data sheet, 192, 212-214
Defaults
Drawing, 228, 240-241
Text, 187
Defining text formats, 160-164
Deleting slides, 60-61
Dissolves, 21
Double-clicking, 204

E

Expanding an outline, 60
Exporting charts, 224

F

Fill patterns, 236-237
Find/Change command, 180
Flip charts, 337, 360-362
Flip frame protectors-3M, 328-
329
Flipping objects, 268
Freehand drawings, 243-244

G

Genigraphics
Preparing files for
transmission, 339-347
Previewing, 347-348
Transmitting via modem,
349-350
GeniLink, 348-350
GeniPeek, 347-348
Graduated fill pattern, 235-237
Grid snap on/off, 269
Grouping objects, 251-254

H

Handouts, 316-319
Helvetica, 129-130
Helvetica Condensed, 326
Helvetica Narrow, 129-130
Hewlett-Packard PaintJet
printers, 329-335
Hide body copy command, 65
Highlighting text, 125
High-low charts, 198

I

Information graphics, 282-290
ITC Lubalin Graph, 326
ITC New Baskerville, 326

J

K

Keyboard shortcuts
    Changing views, 62
    On-screen presentations,
    358-360
    Word processing, 177

L

Line drawing tools, 241-243
Line colors—choosing, 231-233
Line graphs, 196
Line pattern—choosing, 236-
    237
Line defaults, 240-241
Line spacing, 139-141
Line thickness, 102-203
Logo, adding to Slide master,
    91-93

M

Modem transmission, 348-349,
    353

N

New slide, 57
Numbers—formatting in chart,
    208

New Century Schoolbook, 129,
    132
Notes
    Adding comments, 315
    Formatting, 309-312
    Hiding from outline, 314
    Preparing as part of
    outline, 62-65, 312-313

O

Organization chart
    Advantages, 199
    Formatting, 214-217
    Entering data, 215
Outline
    Changing idea levels, 51-52
    Collapsing and expanding,
    59-60
    Creating, 49-50
    Editing, 52-53
    Exporting, 70-71
    Formatting, 67-68
    Importing, 61
    Printing, 68-70
    Reorganizing, 54-56
    Versus speeches, 45-48
Ovals, 249
Overhead transparencies
    Advantages and
    disadvantages, 34-35
    Producing black and white,
    324-328
    Producing color, 329, 335-
    336
    Projector setup, 328-329
    Protectors, 328-329

P

Page number
  Slide, 106-108
  Handouts, 218
Palatino, 129, 132
Pie chart, 193
Placeholder types, 87
Polygon tool, 250
Preferences
  Color quality, 100-101
  Word processing, 176
Previewing
  Before printing, 335
  Previewing before sending
    to Genigraphics, 347-348
Projector pads, 36, 354-355

Q

QMS, 329

R

Reformatting presentations,
  362-365
Regroup command, 254
Resizing objects, 247
Rotating objects, 266-267
Rounded corner boxes, 248
Rules and boxes
  Attributes, 80

S

Scatter charts, 197
Screen fonts, 136
Selecting text, 125, 175-176

Send commands, 264-266
Service bureaus, 338-339
Shadows
  Adjusting text offset, 235-236
  Object, 235-236
  Text, 156-157
Slides—35mm
  Advantages and
    disadvantages, 32-34
  Preparing, 337-339
Slide master
  Applying, 114-116
  Background, 110-113
  Colors, 96-100
  Functions, 14-16, 83-84
  Naming, 109-110
  Placeholders, 88-94, 105-106
  Previewing, 84
  Sharing, 117-118
  Status line, 106-107
Slide orientation, 44
Slide show feature
  Keyboard shortcuts, 358-360
  Using, 296-297
Slide sorter view, 297-303
Slide titles, 50
Spell checker, 178-179
Stacked overlay charts
  Area, 200-201
  Bar, 199-200
  Column, 200
Subtitles
  Adding to outline, 65-66
  Adding to Slide master, 106

T

Tables, 198
Text
    Applying text formats, 166-170
    Attributes, 78-79
    Builds, 181-185
    Color, 174-149
    Defining formats, 160-163
    Editing, 52-53
    Entering, 174-175
    Formatting, 124, 125-147
    Frames, 154
    Selecting, 127
    Shadows, 156-158
    Style options, 137
Text format command, 170
Times Roman, 129, 131
Transition effects, 357
Triple-clicking, 204
Type style alternatives, 137

U

Ungrouping art, 257-258
Ungrouping charts, 277

V

Views
    Outline, 48-60
    Slide, 61-62
    Slide master, 86
    Slide sorter, 297-303

W

Wipes, 21

X

Y

Z

Zapf Chancery, 129, 132
Zapf Dingbats, 129, 133
Zoom command, 269-272